LOUVRE MUSEUM TRAVEL GUIDE 2025

A comprehensive companion that will take you through everything you need to know about visiting, from securing skip the line tickets to discovering the top tours and must-see masterpieces inside.

Clara Rosewood

D1518269

CONTENTS

INTRODUCTION

I remember the first time I set foot in the Louvre. It wasn't my first visit to Paris, but it felt different —almost like the city had been preparing me for this very moment. I had heard countless stories about it, read the histories, seen the pictures. But there's something about being there in person that can't be replicated by any guidebook or travel blog. You stand before the glass pyramid, gazing up at its modern yet timeless design, and suddenly, the weight of history becomes palpable. The Louvre isn't just a museum; it's a portal to the past, a testament to human creativity and ambition, and a symbol of cultural significance that spans centuries and continents.

As I stepped through the iconic glass pyramid entrance, I couldn't help but be overwhelmed by the sheer scale of the place. I had been warned that you couldn't see everything in a single visit, but that didn't prepare me for the vastness of it all. Artworks from ancient Egypt, Greek sculptures, Renaissance masterpieces, and the world-renowned Mona Lisa beckoned me to explore further, each piece telling its own story. The Louvre wasn't just a place to look at art —it was a place where history and culture came to life.

The journey of the Louvre from a royal palace to one of the most famous museums in the world is as fascinating as the artworks it houses. It's a tale of transformation that reflects the changes in French society, monarchy, revolution, and the pursuit of knowledge. What began as the residence of French kings evolved into a cultural institution that has become a must-visit for millions of people each year. The Louvre is not merely a museum in the traditional sense; it's a living, breathing entity, a cultural symbol that transcends its role as a repository of art.

When you walk through its halls, you're not just encountering artwork; you're stepping into a journey of civilization itself. From the ancient to the modern, the Louvre's collections span over 9,000 years of human history, offering a glimpse into the soul of humanity. Whether you're an art enthusiast, a history buff, or someone simply seeking to experience a piece of the past, the Louvre offers something for everyone.

The story of the Louvre is not just about art—it's about the evolution of culture and the impact that art has had on shaping the world. It's about the intersection of politics, power, revolution, and creativity. Every room, every sculpture, every painting at the Louvre tells a piece of this larger story. I often find myself thinking about the people who created these works of art—what were their lives like? What drove them to create such beauty, such meaning? The Louvre connects us to these questions, pulling us into a conversation with the past that stretches beyond the gallery walls.

What I love most about the Louvre, though, is that it's so much more than just a place to admire art. It's an integral part of the fabric of Paris itself. The Louvre's place in the heart of the city, nestled along the Seine, is as symbolic as the treasures it holds. It's an international symbol of art, culture, and history. The Louvre speaks to Paris's deep relationship with the arts, and as you stroll through its galleries, you can't help but feel like you're walking through a living piece of the city's history.

I often think about the first kings who walked the halls of the Louvre, the revolutionaries who fought to transform it into a museum for the people, and the countless visitors from around the world who have walked through its doors since. The Louvre has always been a place of transformation—a place where history is not just preserved but actively experienced. It's a place where the past and the present come together in a harmonious celebration of human achievement.

The Louvre is much more than just a museum; it's a world-renowned cultural hub that has shaped the way we understand art, history, and civilization. With over 35,000 works of art spread across more than 60,000 square meters, it is the largest museum in the world and one of the most important cultural institutions in history. As I stood in front of the Mona Lisa, surrounded by so many other incredible works, I couldn't help but marvel at how much humanity has contributed to the arts. The Louvre, with its awe-inspiring architecture and vast collections, is a monument to that creative spirit.

If you've never been to the Louvre, it's hard to explain the full weight of its significance. It's not just a place to admire paintings or sculptures—it's a place where history comes alive, where art becomes an entryway to understanding the world. Whether you're marveling at the ancient Egyptian artifacts, lost in the intricacies of Renaissance painting, or gazing upon the works of modern masters, the Louvre offers a connection to the past that's unlike any other. Each piece of art tells its own story, but collectively, they weave a tapestry of human experience—one that is rich, diverse, and endlessly fascinating.

So why should you visit the Louvre? Simply put, because it is an iconic piece of French history and a symbol of global culture. The Louvre's status as a cultural hub is a reflection of its long history and its continuing influence on the world of art, education, and preservation. It's a place where you can witness the intersection of history, culture, and creativity. The Louvre is not just for art lovers or historians—it's a place for anyone who wants to experience the essence of human achievement.

For me, my time at the Louvre was not just about looking at art—it was about understanding it, feeling it, and experiencing it in a way that transcended mere observation. It was a journey through time, a chance to witness the evolution of human thought, creativity, and expression. Walking through the Louvre's galleries is a reminder of how art connects us all—across time, culture, and geography. It's a place where the past speaks to the present, and where the stories of humanity are told in the most beautiful and meaningful ways.

Now, let me share some essential facts about the Louvre that will help you prepare for your visit. The Louvre is located in the heart of Paris, on Rue de Rivoli, just a short walk from the Seine River. It's easily accessible by public transportation, with the Palais Royal-Musée du Louvre metro station being the closest. With over 35,000 artworks housed in more than 60,000 square meters, the Louvre is not only the largest museum in the world but also one of the most important cultural institutions in history. Its vast collection spans 9,000 years of human civilization, and it remains an international symbol of art, culture, and history.

If you're planning your visit, I recommend taking your time. The Louvre is massive, and there's so much to see. Whether you have a few hours or an entire day, make sure to immerse yourself in the museum's collections and allow yourself to be transported to another time and place. And when you do, remember that the Louvre isn't just a museum—it's a living, breathing testament to the human spirit, a place where history and culture converge to create something truly extraordinary.

In the end, the Louvre is a place of discovery, not just of art, but of the world itself. It's a place where you can lose yourself in the beauty of human creativity, and where you can find yourself in the process. It's an experience that will stay with you long after you leave its hallowed halls.

CHAPTER 1

overview of louvre

T he Louvre Museum is not just a building, it's a living symbol of history, culture, and art. Nestled along the banks of the Seine River in Paris, the Louvre is the largest art museum in the world, and one of the most visited cultural institutions on the planet. Its very name evokes images of iconic masterpieces, from the enigmatic smile of the Mona Lisa to the graceful elegance of the Venus de Milo, but to truly understand the Louvre, one must appreciate its transformation from a royal palace to a global cultural hub.

A Royal Beginning

The story of the Louvre begins in the late 12th century. Originally built as a fortress by King Philippe Auguste in 1190, the Louvre's role as a defensive structure was short-lived. By the 16th century, the French monarchy had begun using it as a royal residence. Under the reign of King Francis I, the Louvre's status as a royal palace was solidified, and Francis famously invited some of Italy's finest artists, including Leonardo da Vinci, to court. This set the stage for the Louvre's future as a center of artistic and intellectual excellence. The palace itself underwent significant renovations and expansions, with each succeeding monarch adding to its grandeur.

The Birth of a Museum

The Louvre's transformation from a royal residence to a museum began in the late 18th century. The French Revolution was the catalyst for this dramatic shift. As the monarchy fell, the Louvre was reimagined as a public institution for the people, a repository for the nation's artistic treasures. The museum was officially opened in 1793 during the French Revolution, and it wasn't just a building housing artworks; it was a symbol of the new republican ideals. The museum's collection, initially comprised of royal and national treasures, began to grow exponentially, particularly after Napoleon Bonaparte's conquests across Europe. Under Napoleon's rule, the Louvre became the home to a large number of art collections taken from across the continent, further cementing its position as the heart of France's artistic world.

However, it wasn't until the mid-19th century that the Louvre began to take its present shape. It underwent major renovations, and various wings of the palace were transformed into dedicated galleries. With the creation of the Musée du Louvre in 1793, a new chapter in its history began—one that would lead to its eventual renown as the cultural powerhouse it is today.

Architectural Evolution

The Louvre's architecture is a story in itself. Over the centuries, it has evolved from a medieval fortress to a sprawling museum complex, with various additions and renovations reflecting the styles of the times. The most famous and perhaps controversial addition to the Louvre is the glass pyramid at its entrance, designed by architect I. M. Pei and completed in 1989. The pyramid, which now serves as the main entrance to the museum, is a striking contrast to the classical architecture of the Louvre, sparking debates on its modernist design versus the historical nature of the museum. Yet, it has become an iconic feature of the Louvre, symbolizing the museum's blending of the past and present.

The Louvre itself is made up of multiple wings, each dedicated to different periods and styles of art. The Denon Wing houses the *Mona Lisa* and Italian Renaissance masterpieces, while the Sully Wing features collections from the Near East, Egypt, and Greece. The Richelieu Wing is home to French paintings, as well as sculptures and decorative arts. The museum's sheer size, spanning over 60,000 square meters, means that navigating its halls can be a daunting task, but it also means there is something for everyone—from ancient civilizations to modern art.

A Global Cultural Hub

Today, the Louvre is not just a museum, but a cultural institution of international importance. With over

35,000 works of art spanning 9,000 years of human history, the Louvre's collection is unparalleled in its breadth and significance. Visitors from around the world come to the museum to see its iconic pieces, like *The Winged Victory of Samothrace* or *Liberty Leading the People*, but also to explore its more hidden treasures— thousands of lesser-known works that illuminate the history of art and culture.

The Louvre is home to collections from many of the world's most important civilizations: ancient Egypt, Greece, and Rome, as well as masterpieces from the Middle Ages, the Renaissance, and modern times. The museum's collections cover a wide range of media, from sculptures and paintings to decorative arts, textiles, and even ancient artifacts. It's a place where the story of humanity unfolds in rich, vivid detail. The Louvre is more than just a museum—it's a repository of civilization itself.

In addition to its permanent collections, the Louvre hosts temporary exhibitions, educational programs, and special events that draw in millions of visitors each year. The museum is a hub for art lovers, historians, and students, but also for families and casual visitors who simply want to appreciate the beauty and history contained within its walls. The Louvre's public outreach extends beyond the museum itself, with digital projects, traveling exhibitions, and educational partnerships that share its wealth of knowledge with a global audience.

The Louvre's Cultural Significance

The Louvre's cultural significance stretches far beyond its role as a museum. It is an emblem of French identity, a monument to the country's cultural heritage, and a symbol of the transformative power of art. Its collection reflects the diverse cultures and histories that have shaped the modern world, making it a vital part of the cultural landscape in Paris and beyond.

Moreover, the Louvre's significance is tied to its status as a universal museum—one that represents the cultural patrimony of the entire world, not just France. With its collections spanning continents and millennia, the Louvre underscores the importance of preserving and celebrating cultural heritage for future generations. As a symbol of human achievement, it reminds us of our shared history and the unifying power of art.

The Louvre is a testament to the enduring relevance of art in shaping our understanding of the world. It's a place where visitors can experience the achievements of past civilizations, understand the artistic traditions that have influenced contemporary culture, and find inspiration for the future. The museum's role as a beacon of culture and creativity makes it one of the most important cultural institutions in the world.

Getting To The Louvre

The Louvre is centrally located in Paris, making it easily accessible from a variety of transportation methods. Whether you're staying in the heart of the city or exploring from the suburbs, getting to the Louvre is straightforward. With its iconic glass pyramid entrance, you won't miss it once you're in the area, but knowing the best routes and modes of transport will ensure a hassle-free visit.

Directions from Key Paris Landmarks

The Louvre's prime location along the Seine River means it's close to several of Paris's most famous landmarks. Here's how to get there from some of the city's top destinations:

- **From Notre-Dame Cathedral**: If you're staying in the historic heart of Paris, near Notre-Dame, the Louvre is just a short 15-minute walk away. Simply cross the Seine via the Pont Neuf bridge, and you'll find yourself at the Louvre's main entrance, the glass pyramid. Alternatively, you can take Metro Line 1 at *Saint-Michel Notre-Dame* station (just a 5-minute walk from the cathedral) in the direction of La Défense and get off at the *Palais Royal - Musée du Louvre* station. This journey will only take a couple of minutes.

- **From the Eiffel Tower**: A visit to the Louvre from the Eiffel Tower takes about 25 minutes by metro. From the tower, head to the *Bir-Hakeim* metro station (Line 6) and ride to *Charles de Gaulle – Étoile* station. There, transfer to Line 1 and get off at *Palais Royal - Musée du Louvre*. Alternatively, you can enjoy a leisurely 35-minute walk from the Eiffel Tower to the museum, passing by the Champ de Mars and crossing the Seine at Pont des Arts.

- **From Montmartre**: If you're staying in the bohemian district of Montmartre, getting to the Louvre is easy. Take the *Lamarck-Caulaincourt* station on Metro Line 12, travel to *Concorde* (changing at *Pigalle* for Line 2) and then transfer to Metro Line 1 at *Tuileries* station, which will bring you directly to the *Palais Royal - Musée du Louvre* station.

Using Public Transport

Paris's public transportation system is world-renowned for its efficiency, and the Louvre is no exception when it comes to its accessibility by metro and bus.

- **Metro**: The most convenient way to reach the Louvre is by the *Palais Royal - Musée du Louvre* metro station, which serves both Line 1 (yellow line) and Line 7 (pink line). This underground station is located directly beneath the museum complex and provides easy access to the museum's main entrance beneath the glass pyramid. The metro is fast, with trains running frequently throughout the day.

Tip: If you're near the *Tuileries Gardens* (a lovely stop if you're touring the right bank), the *Tuileries* station on Line 1 is just a short 5-minute walk away.

- **Buses**: If you prefer to take a bus, several routes pass close to the Louvre. The most convenient stop is at *Pyramides* (Lines 21, 27, 39, 68, and 95), which is just a 5-minute walk from the main entrance. Alternatively, you can also take the bus routes 72 or 69, which run through the heart of Paris and provide scenic views of the city.

- **Taxis and Ride-Sharing**: While taxis aren't

always the fastest way to travel in Paris, they are still a convenient choice for visitors looking to be dropped directly at the Louvre. Ride-sharing services such as Uber are also widely available throughout Paris, and the drop-off point is usually right at the main entrance of the museum, near the pyramid. Expect a typical fare from central Paris to the Louvre to be around €10-€20, depending on traffic.

Walking Routes from Popular Hotels

If you're staying in a central location, you'll find the Louvre is within walking distance from several popular Parisian hotels. Here are some suggestions:

- **Hotel Le Meurice**: If you're staying in the luxurious Hotel Le Meurice, it's just a 10-minute walk to the Louvre. Simply head east towards the *Rue de Rivoli*, passing through the *Tuileries Gardens* on the way.

- **Hotel de la Ville**: Another centrally located hotel is the Hotel de la Ville, which is a 15-minute walk to the Louvre. Walk towards the *Place Vendôme*, and from there, the museum is just a few minutes away.

- **Ibis Paris**: For those staying at the Ibis hotels located in various central Paris areas, like *Ibis Paris 17 Clichy-Batignolles* or *Ibis Paris Gare de Lyon*, expect a 25 to 35-minute walk to the museum. Along the way, enjoy some of Paris's charming streets, local cafés, and shops.

Accessibility and Special Needs

The Louvre strives to ensure its treasures are accessible to everyone, including visitors with mobility challenges or other special needs. The museum offers a variety of facilities to help guests navigate the galleries with ease.

- **Accessible Entrances**: The museum offers dedicated entrances for those with disabilities, including ramps and elevators. These accessible entrances are located at the *Porte des Lions* (Lions Gate) and at the main entrance beneath the pyramid. The *Porte des Lions* is often less crowded, making it an ideal choice for those who need a more peaceful entry into the museum.

- **Elevators**: Inside the Louvre, visitors with mobility impairments can take advantage of elevators that make it easier to navigate the various wings of the museum. These elevators are located near the museum's entrances and at key points in the galleries.

- **Wheelchairs and Mobility Assistance**: The museum offers free use of wheelchairs for visitors with mobility challenges. These can be borrowed from the information desks located throughout the museum. Additionally, there are several rest areas and seating options available for those who need to take a break.

- **Audio and Visual Aids**: For visitors with hearing or visual impairments, the Louvre provides accessible services such as audio guides with visual aids for the blind and lip-reading guides for the hearing impaired. These services are lable upon request at the information desk.

- **Guided Tours for Special Needs**: The Louvre offers guided tours for visitors with special needs, including tours designed for visitors with cognitive disabilities. These tours are tailored to provide a more immersive and accessible experience of the museum's vast collections.

Websites for Travel Information

For real-time information on public transport, accessibility services, and museum opening hours, the following websites are helpful:

- **Louvre Museum Official Website**: https://www.louvre.fr/en – For opening hours, ticket booking, accessibility details, and more.

- **RATP (Paris Public Transport)**: https://www.ratp.fr/en – For metro, bus, and RER routes, schedules, and fare information.

- **Paris Accessibility Guide**: https://www.parisinfo.com – Provides information on accessible travel options in Paris, including transportation and attractions like the Louvre.

Navigating the Louvre and getting there is easy, thanks to its central location and well-connected transport options. Whether you choose to take the metro, walk from a nearby hotel, or arrive by taxi, you'll be able to enjoy the treasures of the museum with minimal hassle. If you have special needs, the Louvre's accessibility services ensure that everyone can experience the grandeur of this global cultural landmark.

Best Time To Visit The Louvre: Tips For A Smooth Visit

To make the most of your visit, it's essential to plan ahead and consider when to go, how to navigate the museum, and how to capture the beauty of its artwork without hassle. Let's dive into the best times to visit the Louvre and some tips to ensure a smooth, enjoyable experience.

Planning Your Visit

The Louvre is open every day except Tuesdays and

major holidays, which means you'll want to choose your time wisely. The museum houses over 35,000 works of art across more than 60,000 square meters, so depending on the time of day, the crowd can either enhance or detract from your visit.

When to Visit: Early Morning vs. Late Afternoon

The key to a peaceful and enjoyable visit lies in timing. The Louvre, like most major museums, tends to be busiest during the middle of the day, particularly from 11 AM to 3 PM. If you're keen to avoid the large groups and long lines, the best times to visit are early in the morning when the museum first opens or in the late afternoon before closing.

- **Early Morning:** The Louvre opens at 9 AM, and it's ideal to arrive right when the museum opens. During this time, you'll experience fewer visitors, giving you the chance to stroll through the galleries with a bit more space to breathe. Many visitors rush to the most famous pieces like the Mona Lisa, but if you get there early, you can experience these masterpieces without being jostled by the crowds.

- **Late Afternoon:** The Louvre's final entry is one hour before closing, which is typically at 6 PM (with extended hours until 9 PM on Wednesdays and Fridays). In the late afternoon, many visitors start leaving, especially those with children or on day tours, meaning you'll have the museum's halls to yourself. This period is great for a more relaxed experience, with fewer tourists blocking your view of the art and allowing for a more leisurely exploration of the galleries.

The key is to avoid weekends, especially Saturdays, as this is when local Parisians also flock to the museum. Weekdays are always less crowded, so try to plan your visit accordingly.

Strategic Visiting Tips

The Louvre is massive, and wandering aimlessly can leave you feeling overwhelmed. With so much to see, it's helpful to have a plan in place for your visit.

Consider these strategic tips:

- **Start with Your Favorite Wing:** The Louvre is divided into three main wings—Denon, Sully, and Richelieu—each offering a distinct range of artwork. To make your visit more efficient and less exhausting, it's wise to start with the wing that houses your favorite pieces. For example, if you're keen on seeing the Mona Lisa, head to the *Denon Wing*, where this iconic painting is displayed.

- **See the Key Masterpieces First:** If you're visiting for a limited amount of time, it's a good idea to prioritize the museum's must-see pieces. Begin with famous works like the *Mona Lisa, The Venus de Milo, Liberty Leading the People, The Wedding Feast at Cana*, and the *Winged Victory of Samothrace*. Afterward, you can explore the other lesser-known galleries with fewer crowds.

- **Don't Try to See Everything in One Visit:** The Louvre's collections span thousands of years and cover a wide variety of art forms, from ancient civilizations to modern works. Trying to see everything in one visit is not only exhausting but could result in rushing through sections and missing out on the quieter gems in the museum. Instead, consider focusing on a few galleries or periods that interest you the most, and plan your visit over two or more days if possible.

Dress Comfortably

The Louvre is a vast museum with miles of galleries and rooms, so comfort is key. You'll be walking, standing, and exploring for hours, so dressing appropriately is crucial to avoid any discomfort that could detract from your experience.

- **Comfortable Shoes:** A visit to the Louvre will involve a fair amount of walking and standing. Choose comfortable, supportive shoes that will allow you to explore the museum without sore feet. Avoid high heels or sandals that might cause discomfort after a few hours.

- **Layer Your Clothing:** Parisian weather can

be unpredictable, and the Louvre's temperature is kept cool to preserve the artworks, so dressing in layers is a smart choice. Bring a light sweater or jacket that you can remove as needed. Consider a light scarf or a jacket that can easily be carried or stashed in a bag for when you're inside the museum.

- **Bring a Small Bag:** Large bags are not allowed inside the museum, and there's a strict security screening process at the entrances. It's best to bring a small, comfortable backpack or purse with essentials like your ticket, water, and a camera. The Louvre offers a cloakroom service, but keep in mind that larger bags or luggage may need to be checked.

Taking Photos

The Louvre is a photographer's dream, with its stunning architecture and world-class artworks. However, it's important to follow the museum's photography policies and etiquette.

- **Photography Policies:** Visitors are allowed to take photos in most areas of the Louvre, but there are a few restrictions. The use of flash is prohibited, as it can damage the artwork. Additionally, some temporary exhibitions may not allow photography at all, so it's important to check the rules at the entrance of each exhibit.

- **Best Spots for Photos:**

Outside the Museum: The Louvre is as stunning on the outside as it is on the inside. The glass pyramid at the main entrance is an iconic symbol of the museum, offering one of the best photo opportunities. You can take photos of the pyramid itself, or capture the reflection of the museum in the surrounding water pools.

Under the Pyramid: Inside, the glass pyramid is equally photogenic, with its stunning architecture offering an impressive focal point for photos. The geometric symmetry of the glass and the soft light coming through the roof makes for a captivating shot.

With Iconic Artworks: If you're hoping to snap a photo with the *Mona Lisa* or *The Winged Victory of Samothrace*, be prepared for crowds. Timing is everything here, so try visiting early or late in the day when fewer visitors crowd the area around these masterpieces.

Navigating the Crowds

The Louvre, while magnificent, can be overwhelming due to the sheer number of visitors. However, there are ways to avoid the worst of the crowds and ensure a more relaxed experience.

- **How to Avoid Peak Hours:** The busiest hours at the Louvre are typically from 11 AM to 3 PM, especially on weekends. To beat the crowds, visit the museum early in the morning when it opens or in the late afternoon before the museum closes. Weekdays are generally quieter than weekends, so if your schedule allows, plan your visit for Monday, Thursday, or Friday.

- **Secret Spots and Less Crowded Galleries:**

While the main wings of the Louvre, such as the Denon Wing, draw the largest crowds, there are several quieter galleries where you can escape the hustle and bustle. Explore the less famous sections like the *Richelieu Wing* or the *Sully Wing*, which house beautiful collections but tend to be quieter. The *Islamic Art* galleries on the first floor of the Cour Visconti and the *French Painting* rooms in the Richelieu Wing are often overlooked by tourists, offering a more peaceful experience.

- **Use the Museum's Layout to Your Advantage:** The Louvre's design can sometimes work to your advantage. Many visitors flock to the central galleries first, especially those with major works like *The Mona Lisa* or *The Lacemaker* by Vermeer. Head to the more peripheral sections, and you may find you have entire galleries to yourself. For example, the *Napoleon Hall* and *The Apartments of Napoleon III* in the Richelieu Wing are often less crowded and offer a fascinating glimpse into 19th-century French art and history.

CHAPTER 2

Planning your Journey

Visa Requirements and Travel Documents for Visiting the Louvre

B efore heading to Paris to experience the Louvre, it's important to ensure that you have the right documentation in place, especially when it comes to travel visas and other entry requirements. Depending on where you're coming from and your citizenship, you may need to take different steps to gain access to France. Here's a detailed guide on what you need to know about visa requirements and travel documents for visiting Paris and the Louvre.

Do You Need a Visa to Visit France?

France, as part of the Schengen Area, has specific visa requirements for travelers from outside the European Union (EU). The requirement for a visa depends largely on your nationality, the purpose of your visit, and how long you plan to stay.

/EEA Citizens: If you are from the European ɔn (EU) or the European Economic Area (EEA), you don't need a visa to enter France. All you need is a valid passport or identity card to gain entry.

- **Short-Stay Schengen Visa:** If you're traveling from a country outside of the EU and EEA, such as the United States, Canada, or Australia, you may need a short-stay Schengen visa. This visa allows you to stay in France (and other Schengen Area countries) for up to 90 days within a 180-day period for tourism, business, or family visits. The Schengen visa is typically valid for multiple countries, so if you plan on visiting neighboring countries like Italy or Spain during your trip, this visa will cover those as well.

- **Visa-Free Countries:** Citizens of several countries do not need a visa for short stays in France. These include the United States, Canada, Australia, New Zealand, and Japan, among others. However, there are some exceptions, especially for stays that exceed 90 days, where you would need to apply for a long-stay visa.

- **Visa Application Process:** If you need a visa, you will need to apply through the French consulate or embassy in your home country. You will likely be asked to provide documents such as:

1.A valid passport with at least three months' validity beyond your planned departure from France.

2.Proof of travel insurance that covers emergency medical expenses during your stay.

3.Proof of sufficient financial means to support yourself during your stay in France.

4.Proof of accommodation (such as a hotel booking or invitation letter from a host).

5.A round-trip ticket or travel itinerary.

Be sure to apply for your visa well in advance of your planned travel date, as processing times can vary.

Travel Documents for Entry into France

Along with a visa (if required), there are several other

documents you should have when traveling and visiting the Louvre:

1.Passport or National ID Card: As mentioned, a valid passport or national identity card is necessary for entry into France. If you are a non-EU/EEA citizen, make sure your passport has at least six months of validity from your intended date of arrival in France.

2.Proof of Accommodation: Hotels, Airbnb bookings, or a letter from your host can serve as proof of where you'll be staying in Paris. This is often required for visa applications, and also when passing through immigration.

3.Travel Insurance: You are required to have travel insurance covering medical emergencies while in France, particularly for visitors from outside the EU. It's recommended to have coverage that includes hospital care, repatriation, and travel cancellations.

4.Return Ticket: If you're visiting as a tourist, you may need to show proof of onward travel or a return ticket to your home country to prove that you do not intend to overstay your visa or the 90-day allowance.

5.Currency Declaration (for large sums of money): If you're traveling with more than €10,000 or its equivalent in other currencies, you'll need to declare it at customs when entering France. This is a standard requirement for the prevention of money laundering and other financial crimes.

Getting Through Customs at Paris Airports

Paris is served by two major international airports: Charles de Gaulle (CDG) and Orly (ORY). Upon arrival, you will go through customs and immigration. Here's what you can expect:

- **EU/EEA Travelers:** If you are an EU/EEA citizen, you'll pass through the EU immigration control lanes with just your passport or ID card.

- **Non-EU/EEA Travelers:** If you're from outside the EU/EEA, you will go through the "non-EU" lanes and have your passport and visa (if applicable) checked. Be ready to present your visa, return ticket, accommodation details, and possibly your insurance and financial proof. Once you pass immigration, you will go through customs, where you may need to declare large sums of money or certain goods.

Currency And Money Exchange At The Louvre

Once you've arrived in Paris and made your way to the Louvre, it's time to think about how you'll manage your money. France, as part of the Eurozone, uses the euro (€) as its official currency. The Louvre accepts euros for all transactions, including entrance tickets, food, and gift shop purchases. Below is an essential guide to handling money and currency exchange while visiting the museum.

Currency Exchange

- **Euro (€):** The euro is the official currency of France, and it's widely accepted throughout the country. Most tourist destinations in Paris, including the Louvre, will only accept euros for direct transactions. Therefore, it's crucial to exchange your home currency to euros before or upon arrival.

- **Exchange Options:**

Airports and Currency Exchange Kiosks: Paris airports (Charles de Gaulle and Orly) have currency *NO* exchange kiosks where you can exchange your money for euros. However, the rates at these kiosks are usually less favorable than at local banks or exchange services *yes* within the city.

Banks and Exchange Offices: You can exchange money at banks or dedicated exchange offices such as *Travelex* or *Change Group*. These places usually offer better rates than airport kiosks and are scattered throughout the city. Be sure to bring your passport with you, as it may be required for large exchanges.

ATMs: If you prefer to withdraw euros directly, you can use an ATM in Paris. ATMs are widely available throughout the city, including near the Louvre. They typically offer competitive exchange rates, although your home bank may charge a foreign transaction fee. Make sure to inform your bank about your travel plans

check if Chase

to avoid any issues with card usage while abroad.

Money for Tickets and Purchases at the Louvre

- **Entry Fees:** The standard entry fee to the Louvre Museum is around €15-€17 for adults, depending on the time of year and whether there is a temporary exhibition. Children under 18 and EU residents under 26 can enter for free. While the Louvre accepts major credit cards (Visa, Mastercard), it's a good idea to carry some cash for smaller purchases, such as tickets from automated machines or in case of any technical issues.

- **Food and Cafés:** The Louvre has several cafés and restaurants, and while these establishments accept credit and debit cards, it's useful to have cash on hand for quick snacks or coffee. Prices can be quite high inside the museum, so if you're looking to save money, consider bringing your own refreshments or exploring nearby cafés outside the Louvre.

- **Gift Shops:** The museum gift shops also accept

credit cards, but again, cash can be useful for small purchases. The shops offer a range of art books, souvenirs, and replicas of the museum's famous artworks, which can be a wonderful memento of your visit.

Tipping and Service Charges

Tipping in France, especially in touristy areas, is not obligatory but appreciated for good service. In restaurants and cafés, a service charge is typically included in the bill (usually around 15%). However, it is common to leave a small tip for excellent service, usually rounding up the bill or leaving €1-€2 for a small meal or drink.

- **Tipping for Services at the Louvre:** If you take a guided tour or use services such as the cloakroom, you may want to leave a small tip for the staff. While not required, it is a kind gesture to show appreciation for good service.

Final Tips for Currency and Money Exchange

1.Avoid Using Exchange Services at the Airport: As

ned, exchange services at the airport typically offer less favorable rates. Try to change money in advance or use an ATM in Paris for better rates.

2.Notify Your Bank: If you're planning to use your credit or debit card at the Louvre, notify your bank of your travel plans to avoid having your card frozen for suspicious foreign activity.

3.Be Wary of Scams: While Paris is a relatively safe city, always be cautious when exchanging money at street kiosks or dealing with individuals offering exchange services on the streets, as these can sometimes be scams.

Accommodation Options Near The Louvre Museum

1. Le Meurice

- **Cost per Night:** €1,100 - €3,500 (Luxury)
- **Location:** 228 Rue de Rivoli, 75001 Paris
- **Phone Contact:** +33 1 44 58 10 10
- **Website:** www.dorchestercollection.com
- **Proximity to Louvre:** 10-minute walk

- **Proximity to Airport**: 40-minute drive (Charles de Gaulle Airport)

A historical luxury hotel with opulent interiors and world-class service, Le Meurice offers rooms with magnificent views of the Tuileries Garden and the Louvre. It is located just a short walk from the museum, making it an ideal option for those seeking a luxurious stay.

2. Hôtel Regina Louvre

- **Cost per Night**: €350 - €1,000
- **Location**: 2 Place des Pyramides, 75001 Paris
- **Phone Contact**: +33 1 42 60 34 12
- **Website**: www.hotelreginalouvre.com
- **Proximity to Louvre**: 5-minute walk
- **Proximity to Airport**: 40-minute drive (Charles de Gaulle Airport)

This elegant hotel, situated just steps away from the Louvre, blends classic French style with modern comforts. It offers easy access to nearby attractions, including the Musée d'Orsay and the Tuileries Gardens.

3. Hotel Le Louvre

- **Cost per Night**: €150 - €300
- **Location**: 137 Rue Saint-Honoré, 75001 Paris
- **Phone Contact**: +33 1 42 60 31 22
- **Website**: www.hotellouvreparis.com
- **Proximity to Louvre**: 10-minute walk
- **Proximity to Airport**: 40-minute drive (Charles de Gaulle Airport)

A budget-friendly option, Hotel Le Louvre is in a prime location for those who want to explore the city on foot. It is a simple, charming option, with easy access to shopping streets and major attractions, including the Louvre, Notre-Dame, and more.

4. Hotel du Louvre in the Unbound Collection by Hyatt

- **Cost per Night**: €300 - €700
- **Location**: 75001 Paris, 75001 Paris
- **Phone Contact**: +33 1 55 35 37 37
- **Website**: www.hyatt.com

- **Proximity to Louvre**: 5-minute walk
- **Proximity to Airport**: 40-minute drive (Charles de Gaulle Airport)

This elegant hotel blends modern luxury with Parisian chic. Located steps from the Louvre, the hotel features sophisticated rooms, a lively bar, and a chic restaurant. It's a perfect base for travelers looking to experience Paris's grandeur.

5. Grand Hôtel du Palais Royal

- **Cost per Night**: €350 - €900
- **Location**: 4 Rue de Valois, 75001 Paris
- **Phone Contact**: +33 1 42 96 70 30
- **Website**: www.grandhotel-paris.fr
- **Proximity to Louvre**: 3-minute walk
- **Proximity to Airport**: 40-minute drive (Charles de Gaulle Airport)

The Grand Hôtel du Palais Royal, located near the Louvre and Palais Royal, offers luxury, comfort, and a central location. Its proximity to the museum, beautiful gardens, and historical landmarks makes it a prime choice for visitors.

6. Hotel de la Place du Louvre

- **Cost per Night**: €200 - €400
- **Location**: 21 Rue des Pyramides, 75001 Paris
- **Phone Contact**: +33 1 42 60 42 13
- **Website**: www.place-du-louvre.com
- **Proximity to Louvre**: 5-minute walk
- **Proximity to Airport**: 40-minute drive (Charles de Gaulle Airport)

Located a stone's throw from the Louvre, Hotel de la Place du Louvre is a charming, classic hotel ideal for those seeking a central base. The rooms are cozy, with elegant décor, and the hotel is a great option for those on a moderate budget.

7. Les Jardins du Marais

- **Cost per Night**: €150 - €250
- **Location**: 74 Rue Amelot, 75011 Paris
- **Phone Contact**: +33 1 40 21 92 92
- **Website**: www.jardinsdumarais.com

- **Proximity to Louvre**: 25-minute walk / 10-minute metro ride
- **Proximity to Airport**: 45-minute drive (Charles de Gaulle Airport)

If you're looking for something a little further from the Louvre but still centrally located, Les Jardins du Marais offers great value for money. With a beautiful courtyard and comfortable rooms, this hotel is in the vibrant Marais district, close to many attractions.

8. Hôtel des Arts – Montmartre

- **Cost per Night**: €100 - €180
- **Location**: 7 Rue de la Vieuville, 75018 Paris
- **Phone Contact**: +33 1 42 59 57 29
- **Website**: www.hotel-des-arts-montmartre.com
- **Proximity to Louvre**: 30-minute metro ride
- **Proximity to Airport**: 45-minute drive (Charles de Gaulle Airport)

Located in the artistic Montmartre district, Hôtel des Arts offers a cozy, affordable option for travelers. Though a bit farther from the Louvre, it provides an authentic Parisian experience with its charming atmosphere and proximity to iconic sites like the Sacré-Cœur.

9. Novotel Paris Les Halles

- **Cost per Night**: €250 - €450
- **Location**: 8 Place Marguerite de Navarre, 75001 Paris
- **Phone Contact**: +33 1 42 21 60 00
- **Website**: www.accorhotels.com
- **Proximity to Louvre**: 10-minute walk
- **Proximity to Airport**: 40-minute drive (Charles de Gaulle Airport)

Novotel Paris Les Halles is a modern hotel with a prime location near the Louvre and the popular Les Halles district. The hotel offers a family-friendly atmosphere with large rooms, a fitness center, and easy access to the Louvre, as well as transportation links to the rest of Paris.

10. The Westin Paris – Vendôme

- **Cost per Night**: €500 - €1,000
- **Location**: 3 Rue de Castiglione, 75001 Paris
- **Phone Contact**: +33 1 44 77 11 11
- **Website**: www.marriott.com
- **Proximity to Louvre**: 10-minute walk
- **Proximity to Airport**: 45-minute drive (Charles de Gaulle Airport)

The Westin Paris – Vendôme offers a luxurious, five-star experience right in the heart of Paris, just a short stroll from the Louvre. With its elegant rooms and upscale amenities, this is a great option for those seeking the ultimate Parisian experience.

CHAPTER 3

Exploring the Louvre Museum

I n this guide, we'll take you through the layout of the museum, highlighting the three wings – Denon, Sully, and Richelieu – and showcasing some of the most celebrated pieces you'll encounter in each. Additionally, we'll offer a curated experience to guide you through the masterpieces, temporary exhibitions, and the practicalities of your visit, including nearby hotels and resorts for a comfortable stay.

The Museum Layout

The Louvre's architectural grandeur is matched only by its vastness. Covering more than 60,000 square meters and housing over 35,000 works of art, the museum is divided into three main wings: Denon, Sully, and Richelieu. Each wing offers a distinct experience, with pieces spanning different historical periods and artistic movements.

Denon Wing: The Louvre's Masterpieces

As soon as you step into the Denon Wing, you'll be greeted by some of the Louvre's most famous and significant works of art. This wing houses the museum's most well-known pieces, so be prepared to take in some of the most iconic masterpieces in the world.

- **Mona Lisa by Leonardo da Vinci**

  The most famous painting in the world, the **Mona Lisa**, is the crowning jewel of the Denon Wing. Painted by Leonardo da Vinci between 1503 and 1506, the portrait of Lisa Gherardini, wife of a wealthy merchant, has captivated visitors for centuries. The enigmatic smile, subtle use of light, and the serene expression on Mona Lisa's face continue to intrigue art enthusiasts and visitors alike.

  Cost: Free with general museum admission
  Nearby Hotels: Le Meurice (5-minute walk)
  Phone Contact: +33 1 44 58 10 10

- **The Winged Victory of Samothrace**

One of the most impressive sculptures in the museum, the **Winged Victory of Samothrace** stands at the top of the grand staircase in the Denon Wing. This Hellenistic statue, dating back to around 190 BCE, is believed to represent the Greek goddess Nike. Its dynamic pose and the flowing drapery of its wings create a sense of movement, making it a symbol of triumph and victory.

Cost: Free with general museum admission

- **The Venus de Milo**

Another world-renowned sculpture, the **Venus de Milo**, is located in the Denon Wing. Dating from the 2nd century BCE, this marble statue of Aphrodite, the Greek goddess of love and beauty, is famed for its graceful pose and the mystery surrounding its missing arms.

Cost: Free with general museum admission

Sully Wing: Ancient Civilizations

The Sully Wing offers visitors a journey through the ancient world, featuring extensive collections of artifacts from the Near East, Egypt, Greece, and Rome. The architecture of the Sully Wing, originally the medieval Louvre palace, is as historical as the pieces it houses.

- **The Code of Hammurabi**

  One of the most famous ancient texts, the **Code of Hammurabi**, is displayed in the Sully Wing. This Babylonian stele, dating back to around 1754 BCE, is one of the earliest examples of written law and provides a fascinating insight into the justice system of ancient Mesopotamia. The bas-relief at the top shows Hammurabi receiving the laws from the sun god Shamash.

  Cost: Free with general museum admission

- **Egyptian Antiquities: Mummies and Sarcophagi**

  The Sully Wing also contains an impressive

llection of **Egyptian antiquities**, including mummies, sarcophagi, and ancient funerary objects. The collection is one of the largest in the world and provides a deep dive into the burial practices and art of ancient Egypt. Among the most notable pieces are the **mummy of a noblewoman** and the **sarcophagus of the high priest of Amon**.

Cost: Free with general museum admission

Richelieu Wing: The Age of Kings

The Richelieu Wing takes you on a journey through the grandiosity and excess of the French monarchy, showcasing magnificent royal furniture, tapestries, and large-scale paintings. This section of the Louvre is dedicated to the **Age of Kings**, offering an up-close look at the splendor of royal France.

- **French Royal Furniture & Tapestries**
  The Richelieu Wing houses exquisite collections of **French royal furniture** and **tapestries**, many of which date back to the reign of Louis XIV. The

luxurious tapestries depict scenes from Frenc
history, while the intricate furniture pieces reflect
the lavish lifestyles of the French nobility.

Cost: Free with general museum admission

- **The Coronation of Napoleon by Jacques-Louis David**

One of the most iconic paintings in the museum, **The Coronation of Napoleon**, painted by Jacques-Louis David, depicts the moment when Napoleon Bonaparte crowned himself emperor of France. The painting captures the grandeur of the ceremony and showcases David's mastery of the neoclassical style.

Cost: Free with general museum admission

Temporary Exhibitions

In addition to its permanent collections, the Louvre also hosts **temporary exhibitions** that bring new art and cultural artifacts into the museum's spotlight. These exhibitions cover a wide range of themes, nporary art to special collaborations with al museums.

Navigating Temporary Exhibits

Temporary exhibitions at the Louvre are located in designated galleries and are included in the general admission ticket, though sometimes additional charges may apply for certain special exhibitions. It is always recommended to check the **Louvre's official website** for up-to-date information on exhibition schedules and prices before planning your visit.

Some noteworthy exhibitions that visitors often rave about include collections focused on famous artists like **Rembrandt** or **Vermeer**, and cultural showcases highlighting different historical periods, such as the **Ancient Greeks** or **Impressionist masterpieces**.

Suggested Exhibitions to Check Out During the Year:

- **"The Treasures of Ancient Egypt"**
- **"Impressionism and Beyond"**
- **"The Art of the Renaissance"**

Cost for Temporary Exhibitions:

Most temporary exhibitions have an additional entry fee of around €15 to €20, though admission is free for those under 18 and for residents of the European Economic Area (18-25 years old).

Nearby Hotels and Resorts

When visiting the Louvre, it's important to stay in a location that gives you easy access to the museum as well as other attractions. Here are a few nearby hotels and resorts offering excellent comfort and convenience:

1.Le Meurice

Location: 228 Rue de Rivoli, 75001 Paris

Phone: +33 1 44 58 10 10

Cost per Night: €1,100 - €3,500

Proximity to Louvre: 10-minute walk

2.Hôtel Regina Louvre

Location: 2 Place des Pyramides, 75001 Paris

Phone: +33 1 42 60 34 12

Cost per Night: €350 - €1,000

Proximity to Louvre: 5-minute walk

3.Grand Hôtel du Palais Royal

Location: 4 Rue de Valois, 75001 Paris

Phone: +33 1 42 96 70 30

Cost per Night: €350 - €900

Proximity to Louvre: 3-minute walk

4.Novotel Paris Les Halles

Location: 8 Place Marguerite de Navarre, 75001 Paris

Phone: +33 1 42 21 60 00

Cost per Night: €250 - €450

Proximity to Louvre: 10-minute walk

5.Hôtel du Louvre in the Unbound Collection by Hyatt

Location: 75001 Paris, 75001 Paris

Phone: +33 1 55 35 37 37

Cost per Night: €300 - €700

Proximity to Louvre: 5-minute walk

Dining And Resting Areas At The Louvre: Cafés And Restaurants

The dining options at the Louvre and in its vicinity cater to every taste and budget.

Cafés in the Louvre

The Louvre is home to several charming cafés that allow visitors to enjoy a relaxed atmosphere while soaking in the museum's grand surroundings. Here are a few standout spots where you can recharge with a coffee, pastry, or light bite.

Café Richelieu – Sully Wing

Situated in the Sully Wing of the Louvre, Café Richelieu is a charming option for those looking for a quick refreshment. The café's offerings include a variety of pastries, sandwiches, and beverages. The décor is refined but welcoming, and the space is particularly lovely during the warmer months when guests can enjoy outdoor seating with views of the museum's main courtyard and the glass pyramid. It's the ideal spot for taking a break while admiring the Louvre's architecture.

- **Menu**: Coffee, hot chocolate, a variety of pastries (croissants, éclairs), sandwiches, and salads.

- **Cost**: €10-€20 per person.

- **Website**: N/A, as it's directly part of the Louvre's services.

Le Fumoir

Just a short walk from the Louvre, Le Fumoir offers a unique Parisian café experience. Though it isn't technically inside the museum, it's a hidden gem nestled in a lovely space near the museum's glass pyramid. Le Fumoir is a quiet, refined spot offering both sweet and savory items. Visitors can enjoy fresh salads, pastries, and artisanal coffees in a cozy, intimate environment. Its proximity to the museum makes it perfect for a leisurely stop after a museum tour.

- **Menu**: Sandwiches, light meals, French pastries, coffees, and a selection of teas.

- **Cost**: €15-€25 per person.

- **Website**: Le Fumoir

Café Marly – Denon Wing

For those seeking a more luxurious café experience, Café Marly is the place to go. Located within the Denon Wing, just steps from the famous glass pyramid, this café provides not only delectable food but also one of the best views in Paris. Its terrace overlooks the Louvre's courtyard, providing guests with the opportunity to enjoy their food while taking in the grandeur of the museum's architecture. Offering a mix of sweet and savory French dishes, Café Marly's sophisticated setting is perfect for a longer, leisurely break.

- **Menu**: Croissants, pastries, coffee, salads, sandwiches, and fine wines.

- **Cost**: €20-€30 per person.

- **Website**: Café Marly

Restaurants at the Louvre

If you're looking for a more substantial meal after a few hours of wandering the galleries, the Louvre offers a number of sophisticated dining options. These restaurants feature both traditional French cuisine and modern culinary takes, ensuring there's something for every taste.

Le Grand Louvre Restaurant

For a true fine dining experience, Le Grand Louvre Restaurant, located on the first floor of the museum's main building, offers exquisite French cuisine in an elegant setting. Guests can enjoy beautifully presented dishes in a chic atmosphere while enjoying views of the museum's grand architecture. The restaurant's menu features seasonal ingredients and highlights some of the best of French gastronomy. It's the perfect spot for a special occasion or simply to treat yourself after a long day of exploration.

- **Menu**: French gourmet cuisine including foie gras, escargots, duck confit, and seasonal specialties.

- **Cost**: €50-€80 per person for a three-course meal.

- **Website**: N/A (part of the Louvre's services).

Loulou

Located under the museum's glass pyramid, Loulou brings together Mediterranean flavors and a modern, stylish atmosphere. Known for its Italian and French-inspired dishes, this restaurant combines a casual vibe with high-end cuisine, making it perfect for both lunch and dinner. Its beautiful interior and the outdoor terrace offer stunning views of the museum's surroundings, making it a great choice for those looking to enjoy a meal in a vibrant, chic setting.

- **Menu**: Mediterranean dishes with Italian influences, including fresh pasta, seafood, grilled meats, and rich desserts.

- **Cost**: €50-€75 per person.

- **Website**: Loulou

Le Bistrot du Louvre

If you're craving a more traditional Parisian experience, Le Bistrot du Louvre offers classic French bistro fare. Located near the museum's entrance, this bistro is perfect for a quick yet satisfying meal, whether you're after a simple croque-monsieur or a hearty French stew. The cozy atmosphere and rustic décor create a homely vibe, ideal for unwinding after a day of art appreciation.

- **Menu**: Traditional French bistro classics such as onion soup, duck confit, croque-monsieur, and desserts like crème brûlée.

- **Cost**: €20-€30 per person.

- **Website**: Le Bistrot du Louvre

Le Comptoir du Louvre

For something casual but still distinctly French, Le Comptoir du Louvre offers a selection of light bites, from sandwiches to salads, pastries, and coffee. Located in the Richelieu Wing, it's the perfect place to refuel after exploring the museum's ancient art sections. The vibe is laid-back, and the menu focuses on simple, delicious fare that will give you the energy to continue your tour of the Louvre's many galleries.

- **Menu**: Fresh sandwiches, quiches, pastries, salads, hot drinks, and juices.

- **Cost**: €8-€15 per person.

Le Café du Jardin

Located in the Tuileries Gardens just outside the museum, Le Café du Jardin offers a peaceful, outdoor space to relax with a coffee or light snack after your museum visit. With its proximity to the Louvre, it's perfect for enjoying a leisurely break while taking in the beautiful surroundings of the garden. This café is casual and offers light refreshments, making it ideal for a picnic-style experience.

- **Menu**: Pastries, sandwiches, salads, coffee, and cold drinks.

- **Cost**: €10-€15 per person.

La Terrasse du Jardin d'Acclimatation

A little further away, but still within the Louvre's vicinity, La Terrasse du Jardin d'Acclimatation offers a more relaxed, outdoor dining experience in the Jardin des Tuileries. Enjoy French specialties like crêpes, croissants, and hot drinks in an airy and casual environment surrounded by the lush greenery of the park.

- **Menu**: Crêpes, sandwiches, coffee, pastries, and ice cream.

- **Cost**: €8-€15 per person.

Picnic Spots and Nearby Eats

If you'd rather take in the fresh Parisian air while enjoying a meal, the Louvre's surrounding area offers plenty of great spots for a picnic. Whether you're bringing your own food or heading to a nearby café, the Tuileries Garden is one of the most picturesque places to enjoy a quiet break.

Tuileries Garden

Located just outside the Louvre, the Tuileries Garden is one of the most famous public parks in Paris. It's a fantastic spot to grab some takeaway food from nearby bakeries or grocery stores and enjoy it in the scenic gardens, surrounded by fountains, sculptures, and lush greenery.

- **Nearby eateries**: There are numerous cafés and bakeries around the area that sell sandwiches, pastries, and drinks, including **Maison Landemaine** for artisan bread and **Le Pain Quotidien** for fresh organic meals.

Rue de Rivoli

Just a few steps from the Louvre, Rue de Rivoli is lined with cafés and eateries perfect for a casual meal before or after your museum visit. From traditional French bistros to modern eateries, you'll find a range of options to enjoy.

- **Hidden gems**: **L'As du Fallafel**, located in the Marais, is a short walk from the Louvre and serves some of the best falafel in Paris. **Café de Flore** is also a legendary spot for a quintessential Parisian coffee break.

Whether you prefer an elegant sit-down meal or a casual coffee in the Louvre's atmospheric cafés, there rtage of delicious options to fuel your visit. The museum's dining experiences offer a glimpse into Parisian culinary culture, blending traditional French cuisine with a modern, cosmopolitan flair. Whether you're enjoying a croissant at a cozy café or indulging in a gourmet meal under the museum's iconic pyramid, every dining experience at the Louvre is as memorable as the art you'll encounter.

Nightlife At The Louvre: A Unique Blend Of Art, Culture, And Parisian Charm

The Louvre Museum, often associated with quiet reverence and artistic grandeur during the day, offers a completely different experience once the sun sets. While the museum itself may close its doors by nightfall, the areas surrounding it come alive with a vibrant, dynamic energy that blends the essence of Parisian nightlife with the timeless allure of this world-renowned cultural institution. For those who visit the Louvre after hours, a world of exciting opportunities awaits—from exploring the lively cafes and bars in the vicinity to attending exclusive after-hours events within the museum itself. Let's dive into the diverse and fascinating world of nightlife in and around the Louvre.

The Louvre by Night: A Magical Setting

There's something undeniably enchanting about the Louvre at night. As the crowds thin and the museum's majestic architecture is illuminated under the Parisian sky, the Louvre takes on a whole new persona. The glass pyramid, lit up by soft, golden lights, becomes an iconic symbol of Paris after dark, surrounded by the beautifully manicured Tuileries Gardens and the glowing fountains. Walking around the museum grounds at night feels like stepping into a dream, with the sound of footsteps echoing through the courtyards, blending with the whispers of history and art.

Though the museum itself doesn't remain open in the evenings (with the exception of special events), the ambiance of the surrounding areas continues to draw crowds well into the night. The Louvre's location in the heart of Paris, near the Seine and a few steps away chic Palais Royal district, places it in the midst of the city's vibrant nightlife scene. Whether you're looking to enjoy a relaxing drink, attend an exclusive event, or simply take in the sights, the area around the Louvre provides plenty of options for nighttime exploration.

Late-Night Museums and Exclusive Events

On rare occasions, the Louvre itself opens its doors for special late-night events, giving a select group of visitors the chance to experience the museum's treasures in an entirely different light. These events, often held on Friday evenings, offer a unique opportunity to explore the Louvre's vast galleries without the crowds, accompanied by music, art installations, and other cultural performances.

Louvre Night Tours

While regular opening hours typically see the museum close by 6:00 PM or 9:45 PM (depending on the day), the Louvre sometimes offers after-hours tours and events. The museum hosts **Louvre Nights**, which include thematic tours and access to select galleries. These evenings are carefully curated to give visitors an intimate, serene experience of the Louvre's masterpieces. Imagine walking past the *Mona Lisa* or *The Winged Victory of Samothrace* without a throng of visitors crowding around the works.

These tours are typically accompanied by knowledgeable guides who provide fascinating insights into the art and history of the Louvre, allowing guests to appreciate the artworks from a new perspective. The museum also hosts occasional concerts and performances in its grand halls during these evening events, offering a full cultural experience.

Exhibitions After Hours

The Louvre's special exhibitions are another aspect of its nightlife scene. Many temporary exhibitions, particularly those in the *Louvre Lens* (the Louvre's northern branch), offer late-night openings on certain days, allowing visitors to experience cutting-edge art in a quieter, more relaxed environment. You'll often find ticketed evening events tied to temporary exhibitions at the Louvre, which provide an exclusive, atmospheric opportunity to immerse yourself in art.

For those lucky enough to be in Paris during these rare events, the experience of the Louvre by night becomes something unforgettable—a chance to witness timeless masterpieces in solitude, giving each artwork the attention it deserves.

Vibrant Bars and Cafés Near the Louvre

The area surrounding the Louvre is teeming with bars, cafes, and restaurants that stay open late into the evening, making it an ideal location to unwind after a day of cultural immersion. Whether you're looking for a cozy café for a glass of wine or a trendy bar with live music, the Louvre's neighborhood offers a rich variety of nightlife options.

Le Fumoir

Just steps from the Louvre, Le Fumoir is a Parisian classic, offering an intimate, stylish setting perfect for sipping cocktails and enjoying an evening out. The dimly lit bar is a favorite among locals and tourists alike, with its comfortable atmosphere and a menu of expertly crafted cocktails. The bar's vintage décor and relaxed vibe make it an ideal place to unwind after a long day of sightseeing. If you're feeling peckish, Le Fumoir also serves light bites, including delicate French pastries and finger foods.

- **Location**: 6 Rue de l'Amiral de Coligny, 75001 Paris, France

- **Cost**: Cocktails range from €12 to €20

- **Website**: Le Fumoir

Café Marly

Located within the Louvre itself (on the Denon Wing side), Café Marly offers an upscale and sophisticated setting for evening dining and drinks. The café's terrace boasts an incredible view of the Louvre's courtyard and the iconic pyramid. As the evening sets in, the ambiance becomes more relaxed, making it a great spot for a late-night aperitif. Whether you're sipping a glass of wine or enjoying a cocktail, Café

Marly offers a truly Parisian experience that is perfect for reflecting on your day in the Louvre.

- **Location**: Cour Napoléon, 75001 Paris, France
- **Cost**: Around €20–€40 per person
- **Website**: Café Marly

La Terrasse du 1er

For a slightly more modern twist on the classic Parisian café, La Terrasse du 1er is located on the rooftop of the Hôtel The Westin Paris – Vendôme, just a short walk from the Louvre. This upscale bar offers stunning panoramic views of the city, including a direct view of the Louvre's pyramid. La Terrasse is known for its excellent selection of cocktails and its elegant atmosphere, perfect for an evening drink with a view of the Parisian skyline.

- **Location**: 3 Rue de Castiglione, 75001 Paris, France
- **Cost**: Cocktails range from €15 to €25
- **Website**: La Terrasse du 1er

Les Deux Magots

For a traditional Parisian café experience, **Les Deux Magots**, located on Boulevard Saint-Germain, offers a classic Parisian atmosphere with a touch of history. Although a bit further from the Louvre, it's well worth the short walk. This famed café, once frequented by intellectuals like Sartre and Hemingway, offers a cozy environment for enjoying a late-night café crème or a glass of wine. Its chic, historic setting is a testament to the timeless charm of Parisian café culture.

- **Location**: 6 Place Saint-Germain des Prés, 75006 Paris, France
- **Cost**: Around €10–€20 per person
- **Website**: Les Deux Magots

Parisian Nightclubs Near the Louvre

If you're in the mood for a night out dancing and listening to live music, the area surrounding the Louvre offers several nightlife spots where you can enjoy a vibrant atmosphere and unforgettable entertainment.

Le Baron

Just a short walk from the Louvre, **Le Baron** is one of Paris's most exclusive nightclubs, drawing a chic crowd of locals and international celebrities alike. The intimate club has a reputation for great music and a stylish atmosphere, making it the perfect spot to dance the night away in Paris. If you're lucky, you might catch a live DJ performance or a special event. Le Baron is known for its exclusive, fashionable vibe, so be sure to dress the part if you plan to attend.

- **Location**: 6 Avenue Marceau, 75008 Paris, France
- **Cost**: Entry typically costs around €20–€30, depending on the night and event.

L'Arc Paris

Located a bit farther out from the Louvre, **L'Arc Paris** is another luxurious nightclub that's perfect for a glamorous night out. The club's décor is opulent, featuring velvet walls, gold accents, and chandeliers, while the music ranges from house to pop. L'Arc is often frequented by models and celebrities, and it offers an upscale Parisian nightlife experience.

- **Location**: 12 Rue de Presbourg, 75016 Paris, France

- **Cost**: Entry ranges from €20 to €40, depending on the night.

- **Website**: L'Arc Paris

CHAPTER 4

Visitor Amenities & Services at the Louvre

Visiting the Louvre Museum is an unforgettable experience, but navigating such a vast cultural landmark can be overwhelming, especially for first-time visitors. Fortunately, the museum offers a wide range of amenities and services designed to make your visit as smooth and enjoyable as possible. From helpful information desks to guided tours, dining options, and access to Wi-Fi, the Louvre takes care of both the practical and leisure aspects of your experience. This chapter will explore these amenities in detail, ensuring that you make the most of your visit while enjoying the art, history, and culture this iconic museum has to offer.

Information Desks & Maps

The Louvre is massive, with more than 35,000 works of art spread across three main wings: Denon, Sully, and Richelieu. Given its size and complexity, it's easy to feel disoriented. Luckily, the museum has several **information desks** strategically located throughout its premises to assist visitors.

Locations of Information Desks

- **Main Entrance (Pyramide du Louvre)**: The most prominent information desk is located at the museum's main entrance, near the glass pyramid. Here, you can grab a free map of the museum and get initial assistance on how to navigate the galleries. This desk is ideal if you're just entering the museum or have questions about your visit.

- **Richelieu Wing**: Located near the Richelieu Courtyard, the information desk here is handy for visitors accessing this wing, which houses French paintings and royal collections. This location is often less crowded than the main entrance desk, providing a quieter environment to ask questions.

- **Sully Wing**: The information desk located in the Sully Wing near the Cour Carrée is another great spot to stop for help. This area is perfect for those exploring the museum's Egyptian collections or other antiquities, as the Sully Wing has some of the oldest and most important works in the Louvre.

Obtaining Free Museum Maps

At all of the information desks, visitors can pick up **free maps** of the museum. These maps are incredibly useful in navigating the labyrinthine galleries and ensuring that you don't miss out on the Louvre's most iconic works. The maps are available in multiple languages, including English, French, Spanish, German, Italian, and more.

Maps highlight the location of major masterpieces like the *Mona Lisa*, *Venus de Milo*, and *Winged Victory of Samothrace*, as well as exhibitions, services, restrooms, and emergency exits. If you're looking to see specific works, a map can help you plan your route effectively, whether you want to visit a particular section or take a thematic tour of the museum.

How to Get Personalized Help

If you need more specific guidance, the information desks also offer **personalized help**. Friendly staff members are available to answer any questions you may have about the museum, including details about exhibits, galleries, and museum policies. They can also provide advice on the best way to organize your visit, recommend a route based on your interests, and even suggest places to visit nearby for lunch or other cultural experiences. For visitors with specific needs (such as language assistance or accessibility concerns), the staff can offer tailored advice to ensure that your visit is comfortable and enjoyable.

Guided Tours

While exploring the Louvre on your own can be an enriching experience, **guided tours** offer an opportunity to delve deeper into the museum's vast collection with expert insights. Guided tours, available in multiple languages, provide a curated experience that highlights key masterpieces, historical contexts, scinating stories behind the art.

Audio Guides

One of the most popular options for visitors is the **audio guide**. Available in several languages (including English, Spanish, German, Italian, French, and more), these guides provide in-depth commentary on the museum's art and exhibits. Audio guides are perfect for visitors who want to explore the museum at their own pace while learning about the significance of each artwork.

- **Availability**: Audio guides are available for rent at the main entrance, near the pyramid.

- **Cost**: Typically around €5–€7 for the audio guide.

- **Benefits**: These guides offer a flexible way to navigate the museum, allowing you to choose which galleries or pieces to focus on. They are particularly useful if you have a limited amount of time and want to see the most important works.

The Louvre's audio guides also feature thematic tours,

such as "Masterpieces of the Louvre" or "Ancient Egypt," so you can select an experience that aligns with your interests.

Group Tours

For those seeking a more personal and interactive experience, **group tours** offer guided, small-group visits with expert historians and curators. These tours typically last between 1.5 and 3 hours and cover highlights of the museum, from ancient art to Renaissance masterpieces.

- **Cost**: Prices for group tours vary but typically range from €20 to €50 per person, depending on the length and focus of the tour.

- **Booking Details**: Group tours can be booked online through the Louvre's official website or at the museum's ticket counter, though booking in advance is recommended.

Some group tours focus on specific sections of the museum, such as the **French Royal Collection**, **Italian Renaissance Art**, or **Ancient Egyptian Antiquities**, allowing you to choose a theme that excites you most. These tours provide a more detailed understanding of the museum's artworks and the historical significance of the pieces on display. Additionally, many of the group tours offer exclusive access to certain areas of the museum.

Special Guided Tours

The Louvre also offers **special guided tours** that focus on more specific themes or periods in art history. These are ideal for visitors with particular interests or those who have already visited the museum and wish to explore more deeply.

- **Special Tour Examples**: Tours on specific periods (e.g., the **Renaissance Tour**), thematic experiences (e.g., **Art and Revolution in France**), or cultural periods (e.g., **Ancient Egyptian Art**).

- **Availability**: These tours are available by booking through the Louvre's website or in person at the museum.

- **Cost**: Prices for special tours can range from €30

to €70 per person, depending on the length and theme of the tour.

Special tours often include additional perks such as early access to certain galleries, a more intimate experience with fewer people, and a chance to interact more closely with expert guides.

Shops & Cafés

A visit to the Louvre isn't complete without exploring the various **shops and cafés** located throughout the museum. Whether you're looking to purchase a unique souvenir, enjoy a snack, or relax with a cup of coffee, the museum offers a variety of options.

Museum Gift Shops

The **Louvre's gift shops** are not your typical museum stores—they offer an impressive selection of themed books, replicas, and art-based souvenirs. From miniature *Venus de Milo* sculptures to high-quality art books, these shops allow you to bring a piece of the Louvre home with you.

- **Location**: Gift shops can be found throughout

the museum, with the largest shop located in the main hall near the pyramid entrance. There are also smaller shops in the Denon, Richelieu, and Sully wings.

- **What to Buy**: The shops feature a wide range of items, including:

Artistic Replicas: Miniature sculptures, prints, and replicas of famous artworks.

Books: Art books, exhibition catalogs, and guides about the museum's collections.

Souvenirs: Everything from postcards and stationery to jewelry and fashion items inspired by the museum's collections.

- **Price Range**: Souvenirs generally start at around €5, while more elaborate art books or sculptures may cost between €20 and €100.

Many visitors find that the gift shops offer the perfect way to remember their visit and share the experience with loved ones back home.

Cafés & Restaurants

The Louvre has several **cafés and restaurants** where visitors can rest, refresh, and enjoy a meal or drink. These dining establishments are perfect for refueling between gallery visits, or simply enjoying the unique atmosphere of dining in one of the world's most famous museums.

- **Café Richelieu**: Located in the Richelieu Wing, this café offers a relaxed atmosphere where you can enjoy pastries, sandwiches, and light meals. It's perfect for a quick break.

- **Le Fumoir**: A more sophisticated spot, Le Fumoir is located near the museum and offers a refined menu with a selection of French wines and cocktails. The elegant décor and ambiance make it an ideal place for a leisurely lunch or dinner.

- **Café Marly**: Situated just inside the Louvre, Café Marly offers an exquisite setting for dining with views of the museum's glass pyramid. Whether you're enjoying a coffee or a gourmet meal, Café

Marly gives you the chance to dine in style.

- **Louvre Café**: For a more casual option, the Louvre Café offers light bites and sandwiches, ideal for a quick lunch or snack while taking in the museum's breathtaking surroundings.

If you're in the mood for something beyond the museum's walls, the Louvre is surrounded by a variety of **restaurants and cafés** that offer Parisian cuisine. Explore the nearby **Tuileries Garden** for open-air cafés or head to **Rue de Rivoli** for more casual dining spots.

Wi-Fi & Cloakrooms

Visitors to the Louvre also benefit from **free Wi-Fi access** throughout the museum. This service allows you to stay connected, download the museum's mobile app, or search for information about the artworks you encounter. While Wi-Fi is accessible in most areas, it's a good idea to check the available network connections when you enter to ensure you can easily connect.

The **cloakrooms** are another essential service provided for visitors. These are located near the entrance and throughout the museum and offer a safe space to leave your personal items such as coats, bags, or backpacks.

- **Cost**: Cloakroom services are typically free, but some larger items (such as suitcases or large backpacks) may incur a small fee.

- **Convenience**: The cloakrooms ensure that you can explore the museum unencumbered, especially considering that the Louvre's vast galleries require considerable walking.

Visiting The Louvre As A Family Or Group

The Louvre Museum is an awe-inspiring destination, not only for art lovers but also for families and groups looking to experience the beauty and history of one of the world's most famous museums. This chapter will guide you through the best ways to experience the Louvre as a family or group, highlighting practical tips, available programs, and special accommodations for visitors of all ages.

Family Visits

Visiting the Louvre with children or as a family

can be both a fun and educational experience. While the museum is home to some of the world's most revered artworks, it can also be an overwhelming place due to its size and the sheer volume of art on display. However, the Louvre offers several services and activities tailored to younger visitors, making it a great destination for families.

Free Admission for Children Under 18

One of the biggest advantages for families visiting the Louvre is the **free admission for children under 18**. This policy makes it far more accessible for families with young children to enjoy the museum without the concern of hefty admission fees. Children can explore the museum's galleries, from ancient artifacts to Renaissance masterpieces, without worrying about additional costs.

Moreover, **EEA residents** (those from the European Economic Area) are eligible for free admission for young people aged **18 to 25**, making it an affordable cultural outing for university students and young adults.

Special Workshops and Activities for Children

The Louvre is committed to making art accessible to younger visitors, and as such, it offers a range of **workshops and interactive activities** designed specifically for children. These activities can help young ones engage with the artworks in a fun and meaningful way, enhancing their understanding of the exhibits while encouraging creativity.

- **Educational Workshops**: The museum offers workshops where children can learn about the artists, techniques, and stories behind the museum's collections. These workshops are often hands-on, allowing children to create their own art inspired by the works they've seen. The museum offers programs for different age groups, from younger children to teenagers, with a focus on interactive learning.

- **Family Tours**: The Louvre offers **family-friendly tours** that are specifically designed to keep younger visitors engaged. These tours often focus on themes like "The Louvre's Most Famous Artworks" or "Myths and Legends in Art," providing context for key pieces and telling stories that will resonate with younger minds. These tours make the experience educational but also enjoyable, ensuring that kids and adults alike get the most out of their visit.

- **Guided Play**: For younger children, the Louvre offers **play-based tours** where guides lead kids through the museum with fun challenges and games. These activities encourage children to interact with the art and their surroundings in a more dynamic and playful manner.

Child-Friendly Resources and Suggestions

In addition to workshops and activities, the Louvre provides several **child-friendly resources** to ensure that young visitors are both entertained and educated. Some of these include:

- **Family Packs**: The Louvre provides

family packs available at the entrance, which contain interactive materials such as scavenger hunts, quizzes, and other fun activities designed to engage children in the galleries. These materials help kids focus on certain works of art, keeping them engaged while providing educational content.

- **Family-Friendly Areas**: The museum has designated areas for families to rest during their visit. These areas offer comfortable seating and are perfect for taking breaks between galleries. Additionally, there are child-friendly restrooms equipped with changing tables, making it easier for parents with young children.

- **Books and Souvenirs**: The gift shops inside the Louvre offer a wide range of child-friendly books and souvenirs. From art books designed for children to toys and puzzles inspired by the museum's collections, these items provide a lasting memento of the visit while encouraging further exploration of art and culture.

Group Visits

Visiting the Louvre as part of a group, whether for educational purposes, social outings, or organized tours, is another popular way to experience the museum. The Louvre welcomes groups of all sizes, offering tailored services to ensure that everyone in the group enjoys a seamless experience.

Organizing School and Other Group Tours

The Louvre is a popular destination for **school trips**, and the museum offers specialized services to make these visits both informative and enjoyable for students. Teachers and educators can plan group tours that align with curriculum goals, whether they focus on history, art, or culture. The museum's educational department provides resources to help with tour planning, ensuring that each group gets the most out of their visit.

- **Educational Programs**: The Louvre provides programs specifically designed for schools. These programs include guided tours that focus on the historical and artistic context of the collections. They can be customized to the specific interests or needs of the group, such as focusing on Ancient Egypt, Greek and Roman sculptures, or the French Revolution. Educators can also request workshops where students engage in hands-on activities related to the artwork they see.

- **Student-Friendly Resources**: In addition to the educational programs, the Louvre offers **learning resources** such as activity books, worksheets, and online resources that allow students to prepare before their visit. These materials help students understand the history behind the artworks and stimulate their interest in the museum's vast collections.

- **Booking Group Tours**: Booking a **group tour** at the Louvre is relatively simple. Groups can book tours in advance through the museum's website or via phone. It's recommended to book well ahead of time, especially during peak tourist seasons, as group tours can fill up quickly. Prices for group tours vary, but they typically offer discounts for large groups, making it a more affordable way to experience the museum.

Special Arrangements for Large Groups

For those organizing large groups, the Louvre provides **special arrangements** to ensure the visit runs smoothly. Group visits often involve special guides who are skilled at managing large numbers of visitors while ensuring that everyone gets a chance to engage with the artworks.

- **Private Guides for Large Groups**: For particularly large groups, private guides are available who can lead tours tailored to the group's interests. These guides are experienced at managing large crowds and ensuring that each visitor has a meaningful experience, whether they are art enthusiasts or casual visitors.

- **Priority Access and Skip-the-Line Tickets**: Large groups can often benefit from **priority access** and **skip-the-line tickets**, which reduce waiting time at the entrance. This is especially helpful during busy times of the year, such as summer or school vacation periods.

- **Group-Specific Entry Points**: The Louvre has specific entry points for groups to avoid congestion. Group visitors can often bypass the long queues at the main entrance and enter through dedicated gates, ensuring a smoother experience.

Louvre Pro Membership for Frequent Group Visitors

For those who plan to visit the Louvre on a regular basis, especially educational institutions, the museum offers a **Louvre Pro Membership**. This membership is designed for frequent group visitors and offers a range of benefits:

- **Discounted Tickets**: Groups that frequently visit the museum can enjoy discounted admission rates.

- **Exclusive Tours**: Pro members can access exclusive tours that aren't available to the general public, allowing for deeper and more personalized experiences of the museum's collections.

- **Special Events**: Members are invited to special events such as private exhibition viewings, evening receptions, and other exclusive activities, providing a unique opportunity to interact with curators, artists, and other members of the art community.

The Louvre Pro Membership is a great option for educational groups, art enthusiasts, and institutions that wish to engage deeply with the museum's collections over time.

Visitor Experience for All

One of the Louvre's core principles is its commitment to making the museum accessible to everyone, regardless of their abilities or background. The museum has made significant efforts to ensure that people with disabilities and special needs can enjoy their visit just as much as any other visitor. Whether you are visiting with a disability or supporting someone with specific needs, the Louvre provides accommodations that help make your visit more comfortable and accessible.

The Louvre's Commitment to Inclusivity

The Louvre prides itself on being an **inclusive museum**, and its accessibility services reflect this commitment. Visitors with disabilities are provided with several resources and accommodations to ensure that they can explore the museum's vast collections without barriers. The museum's goal is to ensure that all visitors, regardless of their physical, auditory, or cognitive abilities, can have an enjoyable and enriching experience.

Special Accommodations for Visual, Auditory, or Developmental Impairments

The Louvre offers a variety of accommodations for visitors with **visual**, **auditory**, and **developmental impairments**:

- **Visual Impairments**: The Louvre provides **tactile tours** for blind and visually impaired visitors. These tours allow individuals to touch certain objects and sculptures to get a sense of their form and texture. Audio guides are available with descriptive commentary for visitors with visual impairments, making the art more accessible.

- **Auditory Impairments**: For those with hearing impairments, the Louvre offers **sign language interpreters** upon request, ensuring that visitors with hearing loss can participate in guided tours and educational programs. The museum also provides **captioned audio guides** that provide written descriptions of the artwork.

- **Developmental Disabilities**: The Louvre offers **family-friendly programs** designed for children and adults with developmental disabilities. These programs are often more interactive and designed to accommodate sensory needs, providing an enriching experience for all participants.

Additional Accessibility Features

- **Wheelchair Access**: The museum is fully **wheelchair accessible**, with ramps, elevators, and wide corridors. Wheelchairs are available for free at the museum, and visitors can ask at the information desks for assistance.

- **Accessible Toilets**: The Louvre is equipped with accessible restrooms designed to meet the needs of all visitors.

- Assistance for Mobility Impairments: For visitors with mobility challenges, the Louvre provides **personalized assistance**. If you require help getting around, simply ask at the information desk for assistance.

7-Day Itinerary For Exploring The Louvre Museum: An Unforgettable Experience

Visiting the Louvre Museum for seven days offers an incredible opportunity to delve deeply into its vast collections, uncover hidden gems, and fully immerse yourself in one of the world's greatest cultural institutions. With over 35,000 works of art across

60,000 square meters, the museum is so expansive that it can be overwhelming to navigate in a single day. This itinerary is designed to give you a comprehensive experience, balancing time in the museum's most iconic wings, along with a leisurely exploration of its lesser-known treasures. By breaking the visit into manageable chunks, you'll be able to appreciate the museum's art and history without feeling rushed, ensuring an unforgettable trip.

Day 1: Introduction to the Louvre & Overview

- **Morning**:

Start your journey with an introductory visit to the Louvre to get acquainted with the museum's layout, its main wings, and the iconic glass pyramid at the entrance. Collect a museum map (available at the information desk) to help you plan your route over the next few days.

Take a **guided tour** of the museum's **Denon Wing** to familiarize yourself with the most famous works. The **Mona Lisa**, **Winged Victory of Samothrace**, and **Venus**

de Milo are perfect starting points.

- **Afternoon**:

After the tour, explore the **Sulley Wing** on your own, which houses some of the most significant **Egyptian Antiquities**. Discover mummies, sarcophagi, and monumental statues that take you back thousands of years in history.

Have lunch at **Café Richelieu**, located inside the museum, which serves French cuisine in an elegant setting. Take your time and enjoy the atmosphere before continuing.

- **Evening**:

End the day with a visit to the museum's temporary exhibitions. You'll have a chance to explore some of the latest showcases and art displays.

Day 2: Masterpieces of the Renaissance & Classical Art

- **Morning**:

Dedicate the morning to the **Denon Wing**, where

the Louvre's **Renaissance art** collection is located. Marvel at works by **Leonardo da Vinci**, **Raphael**, and **Michelangelo**. The **Mona Lisa** is, of course, the main attraction, but don't miss the stunning **Wedding Feast at Cana** by **Paolo Veronese** and **Saint John the Baptist** by **Leonardo da Vinci**.

- **Afternoon**:

Visit the **Richelieu Wing** and explore the **French Royal Furniture and Tapestries**, and the iconic **Coronation of Napoleon** by **Jacques-Louis David**.

Take a short break at **Café Marly**, offering a view of the museum's courtyard and the Louvre's glass pyramid. Enjoy a coffee or light meal while reflecting on the historical grandeur you've witnessed so far.

- **Evening**:

For your evening exploration, focus on the **Sully Wing**'s **Greek and Roman sculptures**, including **Laocoön and His Sons**. You can also find the famous **Code of Hammurabi** here.

Try some dessert at **Le Fumoir**, an elegant yet relaxed

restaurant located near the museum's entrance.

Day 3: Egyptian & Near Eastern Antiquities

- **Morning**:

Start with an exploration of the **Sully Wing**'s **Egyptian Antiquities** section. Spend time with the **mummies**, **sarcophagi**, and other ancient artifacts, including the **Seated Scribe** and **The Great Sphinx of Tanis**. This is a fantastic chance to dive into Egyptology and learn about ancient civilizations.

- **Afternoon**:

Head to the **Department of Near Eastern Antiquities** in the Sully Wing. Explore ancient Mesopotamian artifacts such as the **Assyrian statues** and the famous **Code of Hammurabi**.

Lunch in the museum's vicinity at **Louvre Café**, a more casual spot that offers a range of French snacks and light meals.

- **Evening**:

Use your evening to focus on the **Louvre's temporary**

exhibitions. These exhibits often cover niche topics, such as **Islamic art, 18th-century French decorative arts**, or **Orientalist paintings**. These exhibits will provide fresh perspectives on history and art.

Day 4: Classical Art & European Masters

- **Morning**:

Explore the **Denon Wing** again, focusing on **classical European paintings** and masterpieces by **Rembrandt, Vermeer**, and **Titian**. Don't miss the **The Wedding Feast at Cana** and the **Raft of the Medusa** by Géricault.

- **Afternoon**:

Head to the **Richelieu Wing** to visit the **Napoleon III Apartments** and view the incredible 19th-century French furniture and decorations. This visit provides a glimpse into the luxurious world of the French Imperial court.

Have lunch at **Le Fumoir**, which offers a more refined experience and a chance to unwind before you return to your art exploration.

- **Evening**:

Focus your evening visit on the **Louvre's lesser-known gems**. Head to the **Sculpture Hall** in the Richelieu Wing to enjoy **Roman and Greek statues**. The **Dying Slave** by **Michelangelo** and **Psyche Revived by Cupid's Kiss** by **Antonio Canova** are stunning examples of classical art.

Day 5: Medieval and Renaissance Art

- **Morning**:

Dedicate this day to exploring the **medieval and Renaissance art** collections. Start by visiting the **Sully Wing** and taking a closer look at **medieval architecture** and **early Christian art**. The **La Sainte-Chapelle** and **Medieval Louvre** displays give you insight into the history of the Louvre itself as a former royal palace.

- **Afternoon**:

Return to the **Denon Wing** and examine **Renaissance artworks** from **Italy** and **Flanders**, including paintings by **Titian** and **Botticelli**. Learn about the **Flemish** and **Dutch** painters, and how their work influenced the

Renaissance movement.

Enjoy a delicious lunch at **Café Richelieu**, offering a variety of French dishes in a quiet and serene setting.

- **Evening**:

In the evening, take a guided tour of the **medieval exhibits**. With fewer crowds during evening hours, this is a great time to explore these more intricate displays.

Day 6: Sculpture & Decorative Arts

- **Morning**:

Start your day by exploring the **Sculpture Gallery** in the **Richelieu Wing**, where you'll find works from antiquity through the Renaissance, Baroque, and Neoclassical periods. Highlights include **The Three Graces** and **The Venus de Milo**.

- **Afternoon**:

Spend the afternoon in the **Decorative Arts section**, home to an extensive collection of **French furniture**, **tapestries**, and **ceramics**. These pieces offer a glimpse into the opulence and history of French aristocracy. Explore **Napoleon III's private apartments** for a more intimate look at the French monarchy.

- **Evening**:

For a relaxed evening, enjoy dinner at **Le Fumoir**, one of the best restaurants in the area, known for its sophisticated menu and intimate atmosphere.

Day 7: Hidden Gems and Special Exhibitions

- **Morning**:

On your final day, take time to explore the museum's **hidden gems**—artworks that are often overlooked but are equally as impressive. Seek out smaller exhibitions, such as **Islamic Art**, **Asian Art**, or **African Art**, which are tucked away in the museum's corners. These exhibits often get fewer visitors, providing a more peaceful experience.

- **Afternoon**:

Take the opportunity to revisit any collections or pieces that you may have missed during the week. You can also spend some time at the museum's **temporary exhibitions**, which change frequently and offer a dynamic selection of art across various periods and regions.

- **Evening**:

For your last evening, enjoy a meal at **Café Marly**, which has one of the most stunning views of the Louvre Pyramid and a great ambiance for reflecting on your unforgettable week of exploration.

Final Tips for Your Visit

- **Pace Yourself**: The Louvre is vast, so it's important to take your time and rest when needed. It's easy to get overwhelmed by the scale of the museum, so don't rush through your visit.

- **Wear Comfortable Shoes**: You'll be walking for hours each day, so make sure you bring comfortable footwear.

- **Check the Museum's Calendar**: The Louvre hosts numerous temporary exhibitions, so make sure to check the museum's website for the latest exhibitions and events to plan your visit accordingly.

CHAPTER 5

Practical Information for Visiting the Louvre Museum

T his chapter covers everything you need to know to make your visit to the Louvre as smooth and enjoyable as possible.

Hours and Admission

The Louvre Museum operates on a set schedule, but understanding its timing will help you avoid the crowds and make the most of your time there.

- **Opening Hours**:
  The Louvre is open every day except for Tuesdays and certain holidays. Regular hours are as follows:

Monday, Thursday, Saturday, Sunday: 9:00 AM to 6:00 PM

Wednesday, Friday: 9:00 AM to 9:00 PM

Closed on Tuesdays: The museum is closed on Tuesdays for maintenance and special exhibitions.

- **Last Entry**:

  For those who wish to explore the Louvre until closing time, note that the **last entry is one hour before closure**. If you're visiting on a weekday, this means you'll need to enter by 8:00 PM if you want to stay until the museum closes at 9:00 PM.

- **Admission Fees**:

  The general admission for adults is **€22**, which grants access to the permanent collections as well as temporary exhibitions. However, there are some exceptions that could save you money:

Free Admission: Visitors under the age of **18** get in free. Additionally, **EU residents under 26** also enjoy free admission. This is a fantastic option for students, families, and young adults exploring Paris on a budget.

- **Other Discounts**:

  Various discounts and exemptions are available, including for those who have disability status, teachers, and other special categories. If you are unsure whether you qualify for a discount, check museum's official website or inquire at the ticket desk.

Tickets and Booking

The Louvre Museum is incredibly popular, and its central location in Paris makes it a must-visit spot for travelers. To avoid long queues and ensure that you get the most out of your time, it's a good idea to plan ahead when it comes to booking tickets.

Online Ticket Booking:
The most efficient way to book tickets is through the **official Louvre Museum website**. Not only does this allow you to bypass long lines, but it also gives you the option to choose your **time slot**. Time slots are available in one-hour increments, and it is strongly recommended to book in advance, especially during peak tourist seasons (spring and summer).

Booking online will give you a specific entry time, which helps in managing the flow of visitors, especially during busy hours. The timed entry system also prevents overcrowding, making for a more pleasant experience.

Time-Slot Recommendations:

The Louvre can get crowded, particularly in the middle of the day. If you're looking to avoid peak crowds, consider booking your entry during the **morning (right when it opens) or late afternoon (after 4:00 PM)**. Visiting on **Wednesday or Friday evenings** when the museum stays open until **9:00 PM** also offers the opportunity to explore with fewer crowds.

- **Ticket Packages and Prices**:

    In addition to standard admission, the Louvre offers a variety of packages that can enhance your visit:

Guided Tours: These tours are available in multiple languages and offer a deeper dive into the museum's collections. Prices for a **group tour** generally start at **€35**, depending on the theme and length of the tour. If you prefer a **private guide**, prices will vary based on your group size and the length of the tour, typically from **€100 to €300**.

Special Events: The museum occasionally hosts special exhibitions, which often require an additional entrance fee. These exhibitions can range in cost from **€10 to €15**, depending on the exhibit.

Louvre+Pass: For repeat visitors, the **Louvre+Pass** offers a series of benefits, including skip-the-line privileges and discounted rates for guided tours or temporary exhibitions. Check the website for availability and up-to-date pricing.

- **Tip**: If you're planning to visit other museums in Paris, consider purchasing a **Paris Museum Pass**. This pass grants you access to a number of cultural sites, including the Louvre, and can save you time and money.

Entrance Options

The Louvre Museum is vast and, especially during peak seasons, lines at the main entrance can be long. Luckily, there are multiple entrance options, each offering a different experience. Here are the main entrances to consider when you're planning your visit.

- **The Iconic Pyramid Entrance**:

    The **Louvre Pyramid** is the most famous and iconic entry point to the museum. This glass pyramid, designed by architect **I. M. Pei**, is not only a striking architectural feature but also the museum's main entrance. Although the Pyramid is symbolic of the Louvre, it can get crowded, especially in the morning and afternoon hours. If you're visiting during peak times, be prepared for longer wait times.

Location: The Pyramid is located in the Cour Napoléon, just outside the museum's main courtyard. It's hard to miss, and you'll be able to spot it from a distance.

Experience: Entering through the pyramid allows you to access the museum's **underground hall**, where you'll find the ticket counters, security checks, and other visitor amenities.

- **Alternative Entrances**:

    If you want to avoid the crowds and save time,

sider using one of the **alternative entrances** to
the Louvre. The museum has a couple of lesser-
known entrances that can offer a quicker, less
crowded experience.

Carrousel du Louvre Entrance:

Located on the lower level of the **Carrousel du Louvre**
shopping mall, this entrance is slightly less busy than
the Pyramid entrance. The **Carrousel du Louvre** mall is
adjacent to the museum and houses a variety of shops,
cafes, and even an exhibition space. You can access this
entrance from **Rue de Rivoli.**

Location: Rue de Rivoli (metro station: Palais Royal –
Musée du Louvre).

Experience: The entrance via Carrousel also connects
to the museum's ticket counter and security check. It
provides a more subdued atmosphere compared to the
bustling Pyramid entrance.

Porte des Lions Entrance:

The **Porte des Lions** entrance is another quiet option,
particularly popular during the off-peak hours. It is

located on the **Seine River side of the museum**, near the **Louvre's south-facing garden**. This entrance is not as frequently used, so it often allows for a faster entry.

Location: **Quai François Mitterrand**, next to the Seine River.

Experience: The Porte des Lions entrance provides direct access to the **Denon Wing**, home to many of the Louvre's masterpieces. However, it may be closed during special exhibitions or events, so be sure to check the Louvre website before you go.

Practical Tips for a Smooth Visit

- **Plan Ahead**: The Louvre Museum is vast, and it's easy to become overwhelmed by the sheer number of exhibits. It's advisable to prioritize the pieces you most want to see before you arrive. Whether it's the **Mona Lisa**, the **Venus de Milo**, or the **Winged Victory of Samothrace**, deciding what to see ahead of time will help you avoid feeling rushed during your visit.

- **Wear Comfortable Shoes**: With over 60,000 square

meters of exhibition space, the Louvre requires a lot of walking. Comfortable shoes are a must if you plan to explore the museum in depth.

- **Use the Louvre App**: The **Louvre Museum app** can help you navigate the galleries and find specific artworks more easily. It provides information on the museum's layout, opening hours, current exhibitions, and even allows you to book tickets directly through the app.

 Consider a Guided Tour: While exploring on your own is rewarding, a **guided tour** can provide deeper insights into the history and context of the artworks. Whether you're interested in **Ancient Egypt**, the **Renaissance**, or **Impressionist masterpieces**, a professional guide will enhance your understanding.

- **Check Temporary Exhibitions**: The Louvre frequently hosts special exhibitions. Make sure to check the website to see if any exhibitions align with your visit. Special exhibitions often feature rare or exclusive artworks, making them an essential part of any trip to the museum.

Safety Tips, Health, And Precautions For Visiting The Louvre Museum

1. Be Aware of Your Belongings

The Louvre, like many popular tourist attractions, can attract pickpockets, especially in crowded areas such as entrances, galleries, or while admiring famous artworks. To avoid losing valuables, consider these practical tips:

- **Secure Your Belongings**: Always keep your bags zipped and close to your body. If you're carrying a backpack, wear it on the front when in busy spaces. Small, secure cross-body bags are often a good choice for keeping essentials like your wallet, phone, and tickets safe.

- **Avoid Showing Valuables**: Try not to flaunt expensive items like jewelry, cameras, or electronics in busy areas. If you're taking photos or videos, be discreet and mindful of your surroundings.

- **Use Anti-theft Gear**: If you're particularly concerned about theft, consider investing in anti-theft backpacks or money belts, which are equipped with locks and cut-resistant straps to deter thieves.

- **Lost and Found**: In case you lose an item, check with the **Lost and Found desk**, typically located near the museum's main entrance or visitor center. The Louvre has a lost-and-found system where items are held for a period before being returned to their owners.

2. Stay Hydrated and Take Breaks

The Louvre is enormous, and navigating its vast halls can be tiring, especially if you're planning to spend several hours exploring the exhibits. It's important to stay hydrated and take regular breaks to avoid fatigue or discomfort.

- **Bring a Water Bottle**: While you cannot bring large bottles of liquid into the museum, you are allowed to bring a small, sealed water bottle. Hydration is important, especially in the warmer months when the museum can get crowded and stuffy. There are also water fountains in the museum where you can refill your bottle.

- **Take Breaks**: If you're feeling fatigued, don't hesitate to take a break. The Louvre has designated **rest areas** throughout the museum where you can sit down, relax, and recharge before continuing your exploration. A quick rest can help prevent muscle strain and make your visit more enjoyable.

- **Eating and Drinking**: The museum offers several dining options, including cafes and restaurants. While it's not mandatory to dine in the museum, you may want to stop at a café for a quick snack or meal. Café Marly and the Louvre Café are popular choices with beautiful views. Eating regularly helps maintain your energy levels throughout your visit.

3. Be Mindful of Health Concerns

Visiting a major museum like the Louvre involves being in close proximity to large groups of people, especially during peak hours. This can increase the risk of catching illnesses like colds, flu, or more serious conditions. Taking simple precautions can help you stay healthy during your trip.

- **COVID-19 Precautions**: While the global situation regarding COVID-19 is improving, it's still advisable to keep abreast of the latest safety protocols for public spaces. The Louvre Museum often updates its health guidelines, which may include:

Wearing masks in crowded indoor spaces.

Using hand sanitizing stations placed throughout the museum.

Social distancing guidelines in certain areas (particularly temporary exhibitions).

- You can check the museum's website or social media for the latest information before your visit.

- **Frequent Hand Washing**: The museum provides numerous hand sanitizing stations throughout the premises. You can also wash your hands in the public restrooms, which are readily available in most parts of the museum. Always sanitize your hands after touching surfaces like railings, display cases, or doorknobs.

- **Sick or Feeling Unwell?** If you feel unwell during your visit, it's essential to take care of yourself. Head to a designated rest area, and if necessary, visit the first aid station located near the main entrance. The Louvre also has on-site medical staff available in case of emergencies.

- **Restrooms and Facilities**: Restrooms are located on various levels of the museum, but they can sometimes be crowded. Take note of their locations and plan bathroom breaks accordingly. Also, ensure that you wash your hands thoroughly, as public restrooms can sometimes be a hotspot for germs.

4. Managing the Crowds

The Louvre is one of the most visited museums in the world, and as such, it can become very crowded, especially during high seasons like spring and summer. The crowds can sometimes be overwhelming, but there are strategies to ensure your visit remains comfortable and enjoyable.

- **Avoiding Peak Hours**: The best way to avoid the worst of the crowds is by visiting early in the morning or later in the evening. Weekdays, especially **Wednesday and Friday evenings**, are less crowded than weekends. If you're visiting during peak season (summer), consider avoiding weekends and public holidays, as these days tend to be the busiest.

- **Crowd Navigation**: If you don't mind crowds but want to see specific artworks like the **Mona Lisa** or the **Venus de Milo**, be strategic about when to visit these pieces. Many visitors rush straight to the Mona Lisa upon entering, so it's often quieter later in the day or early in the morning.

- **Taking Breaks**: If the crowds start to feel too overwhelming, take breaks in less frequented areas. For example, the **Sulley Wing**, which features a massive collection of Egyptian antiquities, can sometimes be less crowded. Similarly, some of the wings like the **Richelieu Wing** are often quieter, providing a peaceful respite.

5. Handling Emergencies

While emergencies are rare, it's always wise to be prepared in case something unexpected happens during your visit.

- **Emergency Contact Numbers**: The museum's main contact number is available on the Louvre's official website. If you're lost, injured, or in need of help, the museum staff is highly trained to assist you. In case of a serious emergency, dial **112**, the European emergency number for medical, police, or fire services.

- **First Aid**: There is a **first aid station** located at the Louvre, staffed with medical professionals who are prepared to deal with minor injuries or health concerns. If you feel unwell or experience an accident, head to the nearest staff member for assistance. You can also ask for medical attention if you feel that your condition requires immediate attention.

- **Fire Safety**: The Louvre, like all large public institutions, adheres to strict fire safety protocols. In case of fire or other emergencies, listen for instructions from museum staff. Evacuation routes are clearly marked in every room and hallway. Familiarize yourself with these routes upon entering the museum.

6. Traveling With Young Children

If you're visiting the Louvre with children, keeping them safe and comfortable should be a top priority. The museum is designed to be family-friendly, but there are a few extra things you should keep in mind.

- **Strollers**: Strollers are permitted within the museum, but some areas, particularly in the older sections of the museum, may be difficult to navigate. If you're bringing a stroller, ensure it is compact and easy to move. The museum also offers **wheelchairs** for visitors who need them, which can be used by families traveling with young children.

- **Children's Activities**: The Louvre offers special **workshops and interactive activities** for children, which can help keep them engaged and entertained. There are also free, child-friendly resources available at the information desks that provide fun and educational activities for younger visitors.

- **Keeping Children Safe**: As with any busy tourist destination, always keep a close eye on your children. Ensure they don't wander off in crowded areas, and consider using identification wristbands for extra peace of mind, especially if your child is old enough to roam but too young to understand the risks of getting lost.

7. General Health Precautions

Finally, while the Louvre is a well-maintained space, it's important to consider basic health precautions while visiting:

- **Allergies and Sensitivities**: The museum contains artworks and sculptures that have been preserved for centuries, some of which may include materials that could trigger allergies. If you're sensitive to dust or fragrances, bring your medication and keep it accessible.

- **Weather**: Paris weather can vary greatly depending on the season. Be prepared for rain during the fall and winter months, and heat during summer. Dressing in layers and carrying a raincoat or umbrella will ensure you're comfortable throughout your visit.

Local Customs And Cultural Etiquette For Visiting The Louvre Museum

1. Respecting Quiet and Calm

The Louvre Museum, as one of the most visited cultural institutions in the world, attracts thousands of visitors daily. With such a high volume of people, it's important to maintain a calm and respectful environment. Many visitors come to the Louvre to deeply appreciate the art, and preserving a serene atmosphere is key.

- **Speaking Quietly**: In the galleries, it's customary to speak in soft voices or remain silent when admiring the artworks. Avoid loud conversations or disruptive behavior that may disturb others who are there to focus on the art. Many rooms, especially those housing famous works like the **Mona Lisa**, can be quiet and introspective spaces for art lovers.

- **Cell Phones**: While it's tempting to take photos and capture memories, always be mindful of your phone's volume. **Keep your phone on silent mode** to avoid disrupting the atmosphere for others. If you need to make a call, step outside or into a designated area.

- **Respecting Personal Space**: As you navigate the museum's busy halls, be mindful of the space around you. Try not to block the view of others who are trying to observe the artworks. Step aside or move to the side of the room if you're taking photographs or examining a particular piece. Personal space is important in French culture, especially in places like museums where crowds gather.

2. Photographing Artworks and the Museum

The Louvre is a visual feast, and many visitors are eager to take photos of their favorite pieces. However, it's important to understand the rules regarding photography and be considerate of others.

- **Photography Policies**: The Louvre generally allows photography in most areas of the museum, but there are exceptions. **Flash photography** and the use of **tripods** are prohibited, as they can damage the artworks over time. Additionally, some temporary exhibits may have strict no-photo policies. Always check the signage near exhibits for specific guidelines. The **Mona Lisa**, for example, is a popular attraction for photos, but avoid blocking the view for others.

- **Etiquette**: When taking pictures, always be quick and considerate. Many visitors will want to have their own moment with an artwork, so avoid lingering too long in front of a popular piece. Don't push or jostle others in an effort to capture the perfect shot.

- **Cameras and Phones**: In galleries with specific rules, like those displaying ancient art or fragile pieces, always look for the signs indicating restrictions on photography. If you're unsure, it's better to ask a staff member. And if you're unsure of whether photography is allowed in a particular area, it's best to avoid taking photos altogether.

3. Dress Code and Appearance

While the Louvre is not as formal as some other

institutions, it's still a major cultural destination and a symbol of French pride. Dressing appropriately is a reflection of respect for the institution and its artworks.

- **Comfort and Style**: Many visitors spend several hours exploring the Louvre, so it's important to wear **comfortable clothing and shoes** for walking. However, avoid overly casual attire such as flip-flops or overly revealing clothing. The museum encourages visitors to dress modestly, and this is particularly true when entering spaces related to religious art or history.

- **Layering for Paris Weather**: Paris weather can change rapidly, so it's a good idea to dress in layers. If you're visiting during the winter, bring a warm coat, as the museum can be chilly in the colder months. During the summer, it can get hot, so lightweight, breathable clothing is a better option. Remember, the museum's large size can make it feel warm inside even when it's cold outside.

- **Consider the Local Norms**: In France other European countries, there is expectation to dress smartly when visiting major cultural sites. While you don't need to be in formal wear, it's important to avoid dressing too casually, particularly for visitors coming directly from the airport or hotel in unkempt attire.

4. Respecting the French Language and Communication

While many staff members at the Louvre speak English, French is the primary language in Paris, and making an effort to understand a bit of French can go a long way in making a positive impression. Even if you're not fluent, here are a few basics that will show your respect for the local culture:

- **Greet People Politely**: The French value good manners, so start your conversations with a greeting. A simple **"Bonjour"** (Good day) or **"Bonsoir"** (Good evening) will go a long way when interacting with the museum staff. If you need to ask a question or request assistance, begin by saying **"Excusez-moi"** (Excuse me) before proceeding with your inquiry.

- **Use Basic French Phrases**: If you don't speak French, try to learn a few common phrases like **"Merci"** (Thank you) and **"S'il vous plaît"** (Please). If you are asking for assistance, say, **"Parlez-vous anglais ?"** (Do you speak English?). While French people are generally understanding of non-French speakers, using basic words and phrases shows respect for the local culture.

- **Don't Interrupt or Overwhelm Staff**: If you need assistance, approach staff members politely and wait your turn if they are already helping someone else. Keep in mind that French people often appreciate a more reserved and formal interaction, so avoid being overly familiar with the staff or jumping into a conversation too quickly.

5. Queuing and Patience

Patience is key when visiting the Louvre, especially

if you plan to visit during peak tourist seasons. The Louvre's main entrance, the **Glass Pyramid**, can become crowded, and the line can sometimes be long, particularly during the summer months.

- **Wait Your Turn**: While the Louvre is a must-see attraction, it's important to understand that everyone is there to enjoy the art in their own time. If there's a line at the entrance or for a particular exhibit, respect the queue and wait your turn. Pushing or trying to skip ahead is seen as rude and inconsiderate.

- **Don't Rush**: Part of the charm of the Louvre is its ability to transport you into another world of culture and history. Avoid rushing through the exhibits. Take your time to immerse yourself in the art, read the placards, and reflect on the pieces you are viewing. If you are on a tight schedule, prioritize the pieces you want to see and save the rest for another visit.

6. Food and Drink Etiquette

While exploring the Louvre, you'll need to stop for food and drink. The museum has several cafés and dining areas where you can rest and refresh, but it's essential to follow the cultural norms around dining in France.

- **No Food Inside the Museum**: It's important to note that visitors are not allowed to bring food into the galleries. You may bring a bottle of water, but picnicking or eating in the museum's rooms is prohibited. There are cafés and restaurants inside where you can enjoy meals or snacks, but these are typically located away from the exhibits.

- **Dining Etiquette**: When dining at the Louvre's restaurants or cafés, be sure to engage in good table manners. In France, meals are an important social event, and taking your time to enjoy your food is appreciated. Don't rush through your meal or be overly loud.

- **Consider Local Dining Hours**: Lunch in France is typically served between **12:00 PM and 2:00 PM**, and dinner between **7:00 PM and 9:00 PM**. If you're visiting the museum during these times, expect the restaurants to be busier, especially at popular spots like **Café Marly** or **Le Fumoir**.

7. Respecting the Museum's Rules and Regulations

Finally, be sure to respect the Louvre Museum's rules and regulations. They exist to protect both the artwork and the visitors. Understanding and adhering to these rules will ensure that you have a smooth and enjoyable experience.

- **Behavioral Expectations**: Running, shouting, or disruptive behavior is strictly prohibited. The museum staff enforces these rules to maintain a quiet and respectful atmosphere for all visitors. Always behave in a courteous manner and remember that the Louvre is a place of cultural significance.

- **No Touching the Art**: It's crucial not to touch the artworks, even if they seem far away or are behind glass. The museum's curators and conservators work hard to preserve these pieces for future generations, and human contact can damage fragile materials.

Faqs For Visitors To The Louvre Museum

Visiting the Louvre Museum is an unforgettable experience, but it's always helpful to know some key details before you go. Here's a list of frequently asked questions that will ensure you have a smooth and enjoyable visit to one of the most iconic cultural institutions in the world.

Can I visit the Louvre for free?

Yes, you can visit the Louvre Museum for free under certain conditions. France offers several exemptions for those who qualify, making the museum accessible to a broader audience. Here's how you can access the museum without charge:

- **Under 18**: If you are 17 years old or younger, you can enter the Louvre free of charge, regardless of your nationality.

- **EU Residents under 26**: If you are a resident of a European Economic Area (EEA) country and under the age of 26, you can also visit the Louvre for free.

- **Disabled Visitors and Their Companions**: If you are disabled or have a companion, entry to the museum is free. You'll need to show proof of your disability.

- **Teachers of Art History**: If you are a teacher of art history in France, you can also access the museum free of charge.

- **On the First Saturday of the Month (October to March)**: During these months, the museum is free to all visitors after 6:00 PM on the first Saturday of the month.

Make sure to check the Louvre's official website for any changes to free admission policies before your visit.

Who is eligible for free admission (under 18s, EEA residents under 26, etc.)?

As mentioned above, here are the key categories of people who are eligible for free admission to the Louvre Museum

1.Visitors under 18 years old: No matter where you're from, anyone under 18 can visit the Louvre for free.

2.European Economic Area (EEA) residents under 26 years old: Citizens of the EU, Norway, Iceland, Liechtenstein, and Switzerland who are under 26 can enjoy free entry to the museum.

3.Disabled visitors and their assistants: People with disabilities and their accompanying assistants can enter for free.

4.Teachers of Art History: Teachers who work in public institutions in France and are teaching art history can also access the museum for free.

Make sure to have valid proof of age or status (like an ID or residency card) with you when entering.

Do I need to book tickets in advance?

While it is not strictly required to book your tickets in advance, it is **highly recommended** for several reasons:

1.Skip the Line: The Louvre is one of the most visited museums in the world, with over 10 million visitors annually. Booking your tickets in advance all to skip the long queues, especially during peak tourist seasons or special exhibitions.

2.Guaranteed Entry: Booking ahead ensures you will have a reserved spot on the day you want to visit, avoiding the risk of being turned away if the museum reaches its daily capacity.

3.Time-Slot Bookings: The Louvre operates a time-slot entry system, and advanced bookings give you the flexibility to choose your preferred time. This ensures smoother entry and reduces crowding inside the museum.

4.Special Exhibitions: If you plan to see one of the temporary exhibitions, booking tickets in advance can guarantee you access to these often limited-time displays.

You can book tickets directly from the Louvre's official website or through trusted third-party services. There are also special passes available that bundle tickets with guided tours or access to other Paris attractions.

Why are time-slot bookings recommended?

Time-slot bookings are recommended to help **manage visitor flow** and avoid overcrowding, which can detract from your museum experience. With a time-slot system, you can choose a convenient window for your visit, ensuring that you enter at a quieter time and avoid the busiest hours. Here's why time-slot bookings are particularly beneficial:

- **Quicker Entry**: With time-slot tickets, you avoid the long queues at the main entrance, especially if you've booked for early morning or late afternoon slots when the museum is less crowded.

- **A More Enjoyable Visit**: By choosing a specific time to enter, you can explore the museum without feeling rushed. It also helps to plan out your visit so you don't miss out on key exhibits.

- **Avoiding Peak Times**: The museum can get incredibly busy during peak hours, particularly around midday and on weekends. Time-slot booking allows you to avoid the busiest periods and enjoy the exhibits more comfortably.

Can I get a refund on tickets?

Ticket refunds are not offered as a general policy, but there are exceptions under certain conditions:

- **Cancellation Policy**: Most standard tickets are non-refundable. However, if you purchased tickets through the Louvre's website or official channels, you may be able to modify your booking (especially for tickets bought well in advance) or reschedule for a later date, depending on the terms and conditions at the time of purchase.

- **Special Circumstances**: In some cases, such as an illness or emergency, you might be able to request a refund or exchange your ticket. This would depend on the specific policies at the time, and it's recommended to contact the Louvre's customer service directly for assistance.

- **Ticket Insurance**: You can opt to purchase **ticket insurance** at the time of booking, which may cover cancellations or delays under certain conditions.

Always check the refund and exchange policy before making your purchase to understand the terms clearly.

Are strollers or prams allowed?

Yes, strollers and prams are allowed in the Louvre Museum, but there are a few guidelines to keep in mind:

- **Space Restrictions**: Some of the museum's galleries may be narrow, and it can get crowded, especially around popular artworks. As a result, some areas may be difficult to navigate with a stroller.

- **Pram Storage**: You can leave your stroller in the designated storage area near the main entrance if you wish to explore the museum without it. Alternatively, you may choose to carry your child in a sling or baby carrier while moving through the galleries.

- **Baby Facilities**: The Louvre has **baby changing rooms** and spaces where parents can take a break if necessary. Always look out for the signs for these facilities, and don't hesitate to ask staff for assistance if you need directions to the nearest baby-changing area.

It's also worth noting that for families visiting with children, the museum offers **family-friendly tours** and workshops, which can be a great way to keep young ones engaged and make your visit more enjoyable.

Other Tips for a Smooth Visit:

- **Bag Checks**: For security reasons, all visitors must pass through a security check upon entering the museum. Expect to have your bags, backpacks, and other personal items inspected.

- **Photography Restrictions**: Be aware of areas where photography may be restricted (for example, temporary exhibitions or certain artworks). Always check signs for these rules and be respectful of them.

- **Food and Drink**: While you can bring water into the museum, eating and drinking in the galleries is prohibited. The museum has a variety of cafes and restaurants where you can take a break and enjoy a meal.

By keeping these FAQs in mind, you'll be well-prepared for your visit to the Louvre Museum. Planning ahead ensures that you get the most out of your trip, allowing you to focus on exploring the art and culture without worrying about logistics or rules.

CONCLUSION

As your visit to the Louvre comes to a close, it's impossible not to be moved by the sheer weight of history, art, and culture that surrounds you. For many, the Louvre is not just a museum—it's an experience, one that stirs emotions, fuels creativity, and ignites a deeper appreciation for human achievement across millennia. It is a place where art isn't merely displayed —it's celebrated, revered, and revered again, as if every painting, every sculpture, every artifact has a story that transcends the walls of the museum. It is a space where time stands still, and the visitor is immersed in centuries of masterpieces that stretch from ancient civilizations to the very heart of modernity.

As you leave, perhaps after hours of wandering through its grand halls or sitting quietly before the Mona Lisa, it's clear that the Louvre leaves an indelible mark on your soul. The experience of being surrounded by the world's greatest artworks—whether they be ancient Egyptian treasures, Renaissance paintings, or the stunning Greek sculptures—is nothing short of awe-inspiring. The Louvre doesn't just offer a collection of objects, it invites visitors to engage with them, to discover their stories, and to experience the creative power that has shaped the world.

The museum itself stands as a testament to the evolution of French history, culture, and the global narrative of art. Originally a royal palace, the Louvre has been transformed over centuries into a beacon of culture, a celebration of artistic mastery, and an emblem of France's commitment to preserving the treasures of the past. It encapsulates the soul of French history—not just in its architecture or its royal past, but in the manner in which it has brought together the best of human artistic achievement from every corner of the world. The works housed within these walls reflect a rich cultural mosaic: they invite you to see the world through the eyes of artists who have come before, and challenge you to think about the world that will come after.

For many, a visit to the Louvre is not just about admiring art. It's about connecting with the very essence of human creativity. Standing before the *Winged Victory of Samothrace*, it's easy to imagine the reverence ancient Greeks had for their gods. Gazing at the delicate smile of the *Mona Lisa*, you may feel yourself drawn into Leonardo da Vinci's genius, wondering what mysteries lie beneath her enigmatic expression. And in the halls of the Sully Wing, as you trace the lines of the ancient Egyptian mummies and read the inscriptions of the *Code of Hammurabi*, you sense the long thread of human history that connects us all, stretching back thousands of years.

The Louvre also acts as a bridge between cultures and time periods. It is a global meeting point where not only French history and culture are honored but also the contributions of artists, thinkers, and creators from across the globe. Its expansive collections bring together artworks from Europe, Africa, Asia, and the Americas, offering a diverse view of humanity's creative journey. From the ancient world to the Renaissance, from Egyptian artifacts to modern art, each corner of the museum is a tribute to the universal language of creativity.

In many ways, the Louvre transcends its role as a museum. It is not simply a place to view art; it is an institution that shapes our understanding of art itself. Whether you're an art aficionado or a casual visitor, the Louvre invites you to become part of its ongoing story. Its collections are constantly evolving, with new exhibitions and temporary displays offering fresh perspectives on old favorites, and rare pieces from lesser-known cultures or periods that provide new insights into the art world.

Moreover, the Louvre's location in the heart of Paris —one of the world's most iconic cities—adds another layer to the experience. As you walk out from the museum into the vibrant streets of the city, you are reminded that the Louvre is not just an isolated cultural institution; it is an integral part of Paris' artistic soul. From the grandeur of the Louvre Pyramid to the charming cafés surrounding the museum, everything about this place is designed to inspire and create a sense of belonging in the world of art.

Visiting the Louvre is not just about ticking off a list of famous works. It's about immersing yourself in the history, culture, and profound beauty that have shaped humanity's greatest artistic accomplishments. It's an opportunity to lose yourself in the timeless world of art and, perhaps, discover a piece of yourself in the process.

So, as you reflect on your time at the Louvre, take a moment to consider how this museum is far more than a repository of objects. It is a living, breathing testament to human achievement—a space where art and history converge, inviting visitors to step into the past, present, and future. The Louvre will always be there, standing proudly as one of the world's greatest cultural landmarks, and you will leave, knowing that part of its soul now resides in you.

It is a place that reminds us of what is truly important:

the beauty of creation, the power of imagination, and the way art transcends time and space, allowing us to connect with people across generations and cultures. Visiting the Louvre is a gift—an experience you'll carry with you, woven into the fabric of your own memories, forever.

In the end, the Louvre isn't just a museum. It's a reflection of humanity's journey through time, a place where the past and present meet to create something timeless. For those fortunate enough to walk through its doors, the Louvre is a pilgrimage of sorts, a journey through the history of civilization and the incredible power of art. Whether it's your first visit or your hundredth, it will always offer new discoveries and leave you with something to ponder long after you've left its majestic halls.

And so, as you walk away from the Louvre, remember this: you've not only visited a museum—you've become part of a larger story, one that stretches back thousands of years and continues to unfold before you.

BONUS

100 "Would You Rather" Fun Games for Family and Friends at the Louvre

"Would You Rather" is a classic, fun, and engaging game perfect for breaking the ice and creating memorable moments with family and friends during your trip to the Louvre. The game is simple to play and can be tailored to your specific location—like the Louvre—making it more entertaining while exploring the museum's masterpieces. The game works by presenting players with two choices, and they have to pick the one they prefer. The more creative or quirky the questions, the more fun it gets!

How to Play:

1.Set up the group: Gather your family or friends around. The game works best with small groups, but larger groups can still play in a fun, interactive way.

2.Take turns: One person asks a "Would you rather" question, and the other players take turns answering.

3.Discuss answers: After each question, you can discuss the answers and why someone might have chosen one option over the other. This helps spark conversation and laughter.

4.Themed for the Louvre: Tailor the questions to the museum's art, history, or culture, making it even more exciting while exploring the museum.

Here are 100 fun "Would You Rather" questions designed specifically for your visit to the Louvre, keeping the theme engaging, educational, and hilarious:

Louvre-Themed "Would You Rather" Questions

1.

Would you rather spend an hour in front of the *Mona Lisa* or in front of the *Venus de Milo*?

2.

Would you rather explore the Egyptian antiquities wing or the Renaissance art wing?

3.

Would you rather live in the Louvre for a
year or work as a guide for a year?

4.

Would you rather have a private tour of
the *Winged Victory of Samothrace* or a
private tour of the *Mona Lisa*?

5.

Would you rather be friends with
Napoleon or Leonardo da Vinci?

6.

Would you rather discover a new painting in the
Louvre or unearth a new Egyptian artifact?

7.

Would you rather have a famous painting named
after you or a statue sculpted in your honor?

8.

Would you rather visit the Louvre at night
under the stars or during the bustling day?

9.

Would you rather take a selfie with the *Mona Lisa*
or with the *Winged Victory of Samothrace*?

10.

Would you rather be able to paint like *Leonardo da Vinci* or sculpt like *Michelangelo*?

11.

Would you rather walk through the Louvre's pyramid or go through the ancient passageways of the museum?

12.

Would you rather study art history for a year at the Louvre or at the Vatican Museums?

13.

Would you rather live in the Louvre during the French Revolution or during Napoleon's reign?

14.

Would you rather have a lifetime pass to the Louvre or the opportunity to meet its curators?

15.

Would you rather be a famous painter or a famous sculptor featured in the Louvre?

16.

Would you rather have the Mona Lisa smile

at you or the *Winged Victory* fly by you?

17.

Would you rather take a boat ride on the Seine near the Louvre or go to a nearby café and people-watch?

18.

Would you rather visit the Louvre during a quiet afternoon or on a busy Saturday?

19.

Would you rather have access to all the hidden rooms in the Louvre or be able to explore the Louvre in total silence?

20.

Would you rather be an art critic for the Louvre or a curator for their temporary exhibitions?

Fun Art and History Questions

21.

Would you rather have dinner with an ancient Egyptian pharaoh or with a Renaissance artist?

22.

Would you rather see *The Code of Hammurabi* or the *Rosetta Stone* in person?

23.

Would you rather be a part of the Louvre's opening ceremony or its grand reopening in 1989?

24.

Would you rather go to the Louvre and see nothing but modern art or only classical pieces?

25.

Would you rather be able to recreate any piece of art or discover an unknown piece of art?

26.

Would you rather paint a masterpiece that will hang in the Louvre or sculpt a statue that will be put in the Louvre Gardens?

27.

Would you rather be part of the Louvre's secret collection or the Museum of Modern Art in New York?

28.

Would you rather go through the Louvre's archives or see a live art restoration in progress?

29.

Would you rather be a part of the *Winged*

Victory of Samothrace restoration team

or a *Mona Lisa* restoration?

30.

Would you rather meet the curator of the Egyptian

collection or the curator of the French royal furniture?

31.

Would you rather walk around the Louvre's

exterior or stay inside the galleries for a day?

32.

Would you rather study an ancient Roman

sculpture or a Renaissance-era painting?

33.

Would you rather view a famous historical

portrait or a modern abstract painting?

34.

Would you rather learn how to draw the *Mona Lisa*

from scratch or craft a replica of the *Venus de Milo*?

35.

Would you rather take a sketching class in front of

the *Winged Victory* or one in front of the *Mona Lisa*?

36.

Would you rather have the Louvre's *Café Richelieu* as your office or *Le Fumoir* as your regular coffee spot?

37.

Would you rather attend a private unveiling of a new Louvre exhibit or a VIP dinner at the museum?

38.

Would you rather visit a temporary exhibit dedicated to one artist or one civilization?

39.

Would you rather have a painting from the *Baroque* era or the *Impressionist* era in your home?

40.

Would you rather see the *Nike of Samothrace* or the *Venus de Milo* come to life?

Playful and Hypothetical Questions

41.

Would you rather time travel to the creation of the *Mona Lisa* or the *Winged Victory*?

42.

Would you rather have unlimited access to the Louvre's archives or the museum's rooftop views for a year?

43.

Would you rather find a new wing of the Louvre or discover a previously unknown masterpiece?

44.

Would you rather have a guided tour by an expert on French Revolution art or by a specialist in Renaissance art?

45.

Would you rather own a piece of modern art or ancient Egyptian jewelry from the Louvre?

46.

Would you rather be an art thief in the Louvre or a secret spy working to protect the museum's collection?

47.

Would you rather see the Louvre stay the same forever or constantly change its collections and exhibitions?

48.

Would you rather see a *Mona Lisa* in every room or only one, kept in the most prestigious room of the Louvre?

49.

Would you rather design your own exhibit
at the Louvre or curate a collection of
art from around the world?

50.

Would you rather bring a famous artwork to life
or have your likeness immortalized in one?

51.

Would you rather spend the night inside the
Louvre or spend a day with no crowds?

52.

Would you rather sit in front of *The Lacemaker* by
Vermeer for an hour or in front of the *Winged Victory*?

53.

Would you rather discover a new historical artifact
or make a groundbreaking art discovery?

54.

Would you rather watch the *Mona Lisa* painted from
scratch or have a live reconstruction of *Venus de Milo*?

55.

Would you rather meet Napoleon or Da
Vinci in the Louvre's Hall of Mirrors?

56.

Would you rather see a replica of the
Venus de Milo or the original?

57.

Would you rather take a hidden path in the
Louvre or be part of the official guide route?

58.

Would you rather dine with art collectors
or museum curators?

59.

Would you rather create art based on
Louvre pieces or create entirely new
masterpieces inspired by the Louvre?

60.

Would you rather be part of the Louvre's first virtual
reality exhibit or a new immersive art installation?

Fun Group Questions

61.

Would you rather see the Louvre transformed
into a grand concert hall or a theatre?

62.

Would you rather explore the Louvre's historical architecture or its art?

63.

Would you rather have a scavenger hunt through the Louvre or a trivia contest about the artworks?

64.

Would you rather take a group photo with the *Mona Lisa* or the *Winged Victory*?

65.

Would you rather have a picnic in the Tuileries Gardens or dine in the Louvre's restaurants?

66.

Would you rather take a yoga class inside the Louvre or a painting class?

67.

Would you rather share a piece of art history with friends or teach them how to paint or sculpt like famous artists?

68.

Would you rather have a competition to see who can find the most famous artworks first or who can discover the most obscure?

69.

Would you rather spend a day at the Louvre or
an entire weekend exploring all of Paris?

70.

Would you rather have an art-themed costume party
inside the Louvre or a French wine-tasting evening?

71.

Would you rather make a documentary about the
Louvre or write a fictional story about an art heist?

72.

Would you rather see your family in a Louvre
painting or on display as sculptures?

73.

Would you rather have a special after-hours tour or
a behind-the-scenes visit to the Louvre's storage?

74.

you rather hold a Louvre art quiz for your family
or a Louvre-themed scavenger hunt?

75.

Would you rather take a painting class at the

Louvre or have a guided tour by a historian?

Quirky Fun Questions

76.

Would you rather see the *Mona Lisa* as a life-size painting or as a tiny, intricate piece of art?

77.

Would you rather have access to the Louvre's secret passages or to its rooftop garden?

78.

Would you rather be an artist featured in the Louvre's collection or be a famous art critic?

79.

Would you rather recreate an ancient artifact or create something entirely new for the Louvre?

80.

Would you rather stay at the Louvre overnight or at a boutique hotel in the heart of Paris?

81.

Would you rather wear a Renaissance-era outfit to the Louvre or a modern-day outfit?

82.

Would you rather spend a whole day sketching the *Venus de Milo* or the *Mona Lisa*?

83.

Would you rather have a souvenir of the *Mona Lisa* or a replica of an ancient Egyptian treasure?

84.

Would you rather discover a famous missing artwork or be able to restore damaged art pieces?

85.

Would you rather have a Louvre art-inspired tattoo or an architectural one?

86.

Would you rather see the Louvre's permanent collection or attend every temporary exhibit?

87.

Would you rather live in an art piece inside the Louvre or have your own artwork displayed there?

88.

Would you rather be the first to discover the Louvre's oldest artifacts or its most modern installations?

89.

Would you rather have your face painted on a Louvre masterpiece or live inside a famous artwork?

90.

Would you rather be a famous art model or a famous art maker?

91.

Would you rather draw your favorite painting inside the Louvre or experience it as a 3D sculpture?

92.

Would you rather be on the cover of a Louvre magazine or have your artwork featured in one?

93.

Would you rather win a competition to design a new Louvre exhibit or restore an ancient sculpture?

94.

Would you rather host a family dinner inside the Louvre or organize an art walk?

95.

Would you rather be a museum director or an artist showcased in the Louvre?

96.

Would you rather see an artist create an artwork in front of you or participate in a collaborative piece?

97.

Would you rather experience the Louvre as a historical landmark or as a modern art space?

98.

Would you rather take a photo with the *Mona Lisa* or have her pose for a painting you create?

99.

Would you rather bring a friend who loves art to the Louvre or someone who's never seen art before?

100.

Would you rather dance in front of a classic painting or create a flash mob near the *Winged Victory*?

Made in United States
Troutdale, OR
05/04/2025

31087061R00100